D1407726

YOUR SIGNATURE LIFE

Pursuing God's Best Every Day

Dianna Booher

TYNDALE HOUSE PUBLISHERS, INC.
WHEATON, ILLINOIS

Visit Tyndale's exciting Web site at www.tyndale.com

Your Signature Life: Pursuing God's Best Every Day

Copyright © 2003 by Dianna Booher. All rights reserved.

Your Signature Life, Your Signature Work, and *Your Signature Self* are trademarks of Booher Consultants, Inc.

Cover photograph copyright © 2003 by ImageState/electraVision/PictureQuest. All rights reserved.

Designed by Beth Sparkman

Published in association with the literary agency of Alive Communications, Inc., 7680 Goddard Street, Suite 200, Colorado Springs, CO 80920.

The story at the beginning of chapter 8 first appeared in *Well Connected: Power Your Own Soul by Plugging into Others* by Dianna Booher (Nashville: Word Publishing, 2002).

Many of the quotations used in this book were taken from *Quotable Quotations,* compiled by Lloyd Cory (Wheaton, Ill.: Victor Books, 1985) and from *14,000 Quips & Quotes for Writers and Speakers,* compiled by E. C. McKenzie (Grand Rapids, Baker Books, 1984).

Information from the survey on moral choices (pages 15–16) used by permission of Barna Research Group, Ventura, California (www.barna.org).

Information from the survey on personal success (page 279) used by permission of Barna Research Group, Ventura California (www.barna.org).

Unless otherwise indicated, all Scripture quotations are taken from the *Holy Bible,* New International Version®. NIV®. Copyright © 1973, 1978, 1984 by International Bible Society. Used by permission of Zondervan Publishing House. All rights reserved.

Scripture quotations marked TLB are taken from *The Living Bible,* copyright © 1971. Used by permission of Tyndale House Publishers, Inc., Wheaton, Illinois 60189. All rights reserved.

Scripture quotations marked NLT are taken from the *Holy Bible,* New Living Translation, copyright © 1996. Used by permission of Tyndale House Publishers, Inc., Wheaton, Illinois 60189. All rights reserved.

Scripture quotations marked NASB are taken from the *New American Standard Bible,* © 1960, 1962, 1963, 1968, 1971, 1972, 1973, 1975, 1977 by The Lockman Foundation. Used by permission.

Scripture quotations marked "NKJV" are taken from the New King James Version. Copyright © 1979, 1980, 1982, 1991 by Thomas Nelson, Inc. Used by permission. All rights reserved.

Scripture quotations marked KJV are taken from the *Holy Bible,* King James Version.

Scripture quotations marked ICB are taken from the *International Children's Bible, New Century Version,* copyright © 1986, 1988 by Word Publishing, Dallas, Texas 75039. Used by permission.

Library of Congress Cataloging-in-Publication Data

Booher, Dianna.
  Your signatue life : pursuing God's best every day / Dianna Booher.
    p. cm.
  ISBN 0-8423-8280-1
1. Conduct of life. 2. Spiritual life—Christianity. I. Title.
BJ1581.2 .B62 2003
248.4—dc21   2003012095

Printed in the United States of America

09 08 07 06 05 04 03
7   6   5   4   3   2   1

CONTENTS

ACKNOWLEDGMENTS

Every book, like every life, is a collaborative effort. This book is no exception. The ideas here have been collected from the people with whom I've worked and lived for many years.

First, my parents, Alton and Opal Daniels, for the opportunity to observe their character in action and for modeling all the principles in this book.

To the "cast of characters" in my own life story: Vernon Rae, Jeff Booher, Jennifer Booher, Courtney Booher, Grant Booher, Jake Booher, Lisa Booher McGown, Kevin McGown, Mason McGown, Elena McGown, Spencer McGown.

To the staff at Booher Consultants: It would be difficult to find a group of more dedicated, productive, loving employees than those we have working to accomplish our communication training, speaking, and writing goals.

I would like to thank several people specifically for their efforts on this book:

Polly Fuhrman, Anita Slusher, and Amy Wicke for their very capable research efforts;

Jeff Booher, Sally Luttrell, and Eric Anderson for their keen editorial eyes;

Kim Collins and Lisa McGown, for reviewing my art analogies in part 3;

Greg Johnson, my literary agent, for his encouragement in my work through the years;

Tammy Faxel and Ramona Cramer Tucker, our editors at Tyndale, who immediately caught the vision for this book.

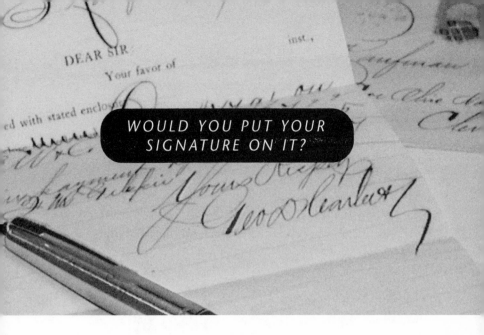

WOULD YOU PUT YOUR SIGNATURE ON IT?

What if we all lived each day of our lives in such a way that we would be proud to add our signature to it when the day was over—just as the artist, novelist, or clothing designer signs a finished piece of work? When artisans sign their work, they're making a statement: "I'm taking ownership. This is my personal best at this moment."

It has been said that your life is God's gift to you. What you make of it is your gift to God. That being the case, you are responsible for designing a life that will honor God. In that sense, you are the creator of your character, the writer of your life's story, and the architect of your work life. Your body is the temple of God, and he can live either in a small motel room or a mansion, depending on your intention and the attention you give to what kind of life you are building by the way you live each day. This book will take you through the facets of building Your Signature Life—that is, a life that you will be happy to sign your name to every evening.

In part 1, Your Signature Self, you'll visualize yourself as a painter creating a great masterpiece in order to focus on traits that form your character portrait. Honesty, wisdom, determination, courage, compassion, loyalty, and faith—these traits must continue to develop and grow as a basis for maintaining your personal best in all other areas of your life. Like the foundation of your house, it is essential that this core layer of character be strong and solidly developed if you are to be able to live out Your Signature Life in your relationships and your workplace.

Your Signature Relationships (part 2) puts you in the role of scriptwriter or novelist, creating your own life story. You'll examine the principles upon which all good relationships function, whether they're parent-child relationships, friendships, marriages, or work relationships.

You may be struggling in a bad relationship and ready to give up. You may want to make a good relationship even stronger so that it can withstand storms (tragedy, illness, separation, disappointment, and sometimes prosperity) when they hit—and they *will* hit. You may want to begin a new relationship—with someone who doesn't yet know that you exist or with someone who may need your influence desperately but resists it for some reason. Part 2 will give you tools to help you build Your Signature Relationships.

Your Signature Work (part 3) uses the analogy of building a dream home as it relates to understanding your work as a calling to serve God and others. It approaches your work—whether in a career, in volunteer projects, or in the home—as an avenue to influence and lead others. Part 3 discusses questions and issues such as these: You may go to work every day unhappy in your job and unmotivated to do a good job because you don't see any lasting purpose to it. You may see no connection between your spiritual life and your work at home or in the marketplace. You may not realize how much the Bible has to say about your work life and habits. You may be frustrated by the lack of integrity you see all around you and want to know how you can change that situation.

Of course, when you build a house, you don't build it room by room. You don't build the kitchen, then go back and build all the bedrooms, followed by a family room, the bathrooms, and finally all the closets. Instead, you plan the house as an integrated project from the beginning, and you work on several similar tasks in many areas at once. First you lay the foundation for the entire house. Then you frame all the rooms. Then you run the plumbing lines and the electrical wiring for the entire house. And finally, weeks or months later, you are ready to paint the entire house and move in.

The same is true of building a life. Compartmentalizing doesn't work very well. You may have heard friends say, "The first two years I'll spend on my marriage. The next decade or two I'll focus on my career. Then in the third decade, I'm going to spend some time in the community. And when I retire, I'm going to have plenty of time to volunteer and serve others and work on me. I want to read and go back to school and. . . ." Their list for self-improvement goes on and on.

But like painting a portrait, writing a blockbuster, or building a house, building a life comes much easier when you tackle it as a unified project: growing your character while you're on the job, strengthening relationships and influencing others while you work in the community, becoming a better mother as you struggle with an ethical dilemma your committee faces, building a closer friendship as you work through a job difficulty with your boss or client, serving God through the opportunities you gain from recognition at work.

Self. Relationships. Work. Parts of one integrated, balanced life. As you work on creating this masterpiece called your life, you'll want to be able to say you've done your personal best so that you can sign your name to what you have lived.

Ready for reflection on your work in progress? Your Signature Life—let's work on building ours together.

—Dianna Booher

PART ONE

YOUR SIGNATURE
SELF . . .

like painting a portrait

*I*n the 1916 classic autobiographical novel *A Portrait of the Artist as a Young Man*, author James Joyce tells of an artist who has his portrait painted in his youth. Over the course of his life as the young man's character changes, so does the portrait, until it becomes a hideous depiction of his soul as reflected in his face. Though the story is surreal, the phenomenon can be quite true in every person's life.

You do become the artist who paints your own portrait from the inside out—your character. You paint it habit by habit, day by day, line by line, shadow upon shadow. Each conversation you have adds its own color to the canvas. Each dilemma carves a new dimension. Every decision creates new depth. Failures and successes give perspective. Over time, each trait blends into the final character profile.

The canvas is yours. Your character is ready for your creation. It will be your most priceless possession. You have final say about what goes into it. After you've completed it, no one can destroy it or alter it. Once you sign your name to it and leave your earthly studio, you will always be remembered by this final, distinctive work of art.

Fame is vapor; popularity an accident; riches take wings. Only one thing endures and that is character.

—HORACE GREELEY

Character gives splendor to youth and awe to wrinkled skin and gray hairs.   —RALPH WALDO EMERSON

Character is not made in a crisis—it is only exhibited.

—ROBERT FREEMAN

Conflict is the main ingredient in God's character development program.   —ERWIN W. LUTZER

A man's character, like rich topsoil, can erode so gradually you don't notice till it's gone.

—*COUNTRY PARSON,* COMPILED BY LLOYD CORY

Man looks at the outward appearance, but the Lord looks at the heart.   —1 SAMUEL 16:7

We must never put character in the place of faith. Our character can never be meritorious before God; we stand before God on the basis of his grace. Character is the evidence that we are built on the right foundation.

—OSWALD CHAMBERS

I'm not happy, I'm cheerful. There's a difference. A happy woman has no cares at all. A cheerful woman has cares but has learned how to deal with them.   —BEVERLY SILLS

HONESTY
Working through the Shades of Gray

$\mathcal{H}$ow honest are you?

WOULD you be embarrassed if your family and friends saw a videotape of your previous year—24/7?

From the time artists begin studying their craft, they concern themselves with the "values" of colors. For example, pure white may have a value of ten and pure black a value of one, with many shades (and values) of gray in between. If artists continue to dilute or add a different pigment to a particular color, they will no longer be able to identify the original color. Whether they are working in pastels, oils, or watercolors, it is a great challenge for artists to keep their colors true and pure. No artist wants to end up with "mud," a noncolor. When something contaminates the purity of the color, the artist has to start over.

Portrait artists also must stay true to their subject. In the process of sketching the basic lines and adding and blending color and shading, it may become tempting to leave out a slight blemish, straighten a nose, or flatten the ears to make the final portrait "better." The artist may think the change is only a slight one, but those who know the subject of the portrait will immediately recognize that something isn't quite right.

The same process occurs where honesty is concerned. Most people start with a "pure" idea of what honesty is and distinct lines around things they consider dishonest: lying, stealing, or marital infidelity, for example. But then something happens to dilute, shade, or discolor these lines. The once clear picture of what honesty looks like begins to fade and becomes gray, then grayer, and finally invisible to the naked eye. The idea of honesty is no longer a clear, distinctive habit or character trait, and now the once clearly wrong action looks unclear and muddy.

Corporate America has spawned a myriad of managers who say to employees, "Do what you have to do—just don't tell me about it." They aren't above breaking the rules to achieve a goal, but they want to feel guilt-free if a subordinate's methods are less than moral. Pity the poor person who must try to walk the tightrope between producing results and protecting a manager's conscience.

Even parents get caught up in this focus on facade. To "Johnny" or "Jordan" Mom or Dad may yell, "I'd better not catch you sneaking the car out with your friends when we're gone for the weekend" or "Don't let me catch you cheating on a test, or you'll be grounded for a month!" Although parents may intend to curb a child's tendency toward dishonesty, their language in such warnings places the focus on not being "caught" rather than on being honest in the first place. As a result, many people come to adulthood measuring honesty by this standard: What can I do "under the radar screen"? In other words, how much can I get away with?

*The measure of a man's real character is what he would
do if he knew he never would be found out.*
—THOMAS BABINGTON MACAULAY

*The essence of greatness is the perception that virtue
is enough.* —RALPH WALDO EMERSON

WHERE WERE YOU WHEN THE LIGHTS WENT OUT?

One of the great irritations about living in small-town America
is that everybody seems to know everybody else's business. And
one of the great benefits of living in small-town America is that
everybody knows everybody's business. Remember the jubilation
of the entire town of Palestine, West Virginia, over the safe return
of POW Jessica Lynch from the war in Iraq? The people in her
hometown all knew her personally. If you happened to grow up
in a small town, you probably understand what I mean when
I say that if you didn't toe the line, it wasn't long before your
parents heard the news. Every other parent, neighbor, or teacher
felt an obligation to report your shenanigans to your parents
so they could punish you and get you back on the straight and
narrow path.

The reverse seems more the climate today—for both children
and adults: more anonymity, less visibility, and less accountability. Rather than congregate on the front porches of the past
in rural America, we often live in suburbia where we frequently
don't know our neighbors. We've moved to the back porch,
put up fences, and shut ourselves off from those who live next
to us or across the street. The neighbors could be hosting wild
orgies, burying bodies in the backyard, or selling magic potions

microwaved in their kitchen without fear of discovery for days or maybe even decades.

Technology has also contributed to the feeling of anonymity and the lack of accountability. The fact that we have tele-commuters who rarely see their coworkers, bosses who manage companies from across the country, customers who buy on-line, and clients who interact with us only by phone or e-mail makes it easier to hide dishonest practices. After all, by the time bosses, clients, or coworkers actually see the results of their actions in given situations, the individual responsible for the consequences may already have moved out of the job. When we routinely deal with people at arm's length, it's easier to feel guilt-free about shabby or dishonest treatment.

Frequent travel, too, has put temptation in the path of many professionals. After all, the reasoning goes, who will know what I do when I'm alone on the road?

In many cases, leaders have set the example for dishonest dealings—from those at Enron, WorldCom, Tyco, Adelphia, Conseco, and Arthur Andersen to those holding the highest political offices. Ernst & Young LLP recently reported the findings from its eighth global study on corporate fraud, a survey of views among senior executives of top corporations around the world. The study found that 47 percent of these corporations were significantly affected by fraud in the past year, and 85 percent of the worst cases of fraud were committed by their own employees, over half of them from the ranks of management. When others see these people "get away with it," they often begin to think, *If they can do it and still get into office or "get out of jail free," nothing bad will happen to me either.*

College students are watching all of this closely. According to an article in the December 9, 2002 issue of *Business Week*, 77 percent of those surveyed about the rash of corporate scandals said they think CEOs should be held personally responsible for wrongdoing in their companies. In response to questions about their own ethics, however, 59 percent of the students admitted to cheating on an exam, and only 19 percent said they would report a classmate who cheated. Clearly, the majority of those students are following in the tracks left by the most visible dishonest corporate and political leaders.

Finally, our culture as a whole has tended to take on a blame-the-victim mentality: Have you ever heard someone comment, "She was asking for it—why was she wearing jewelry like that on the street at that hour?" "He should have known better than to use such an obvious password." "Why was he carrying that much cash? That was stupid." "The company should have better checks and balances in place to prevent that kind of thing." "What did management expect with employees under such stress? They are going to take days off any way they can get them—legally or illegally." "Organizations who can't do better than that with security deserve to be hacked."

Just because the bright lights of honesty have been dimming or have gone out in some organizations—and anonymity seems to remove accountability—we shouldn't be fooled. Sooner or later the lights will come back on, and the level of responsibility and accountability will show up clearly in the final character portrait.

Perhaps the straight and narrow path would be wide if more people used it.
                                        —KAY INGRAM

DISCOLORATIONS IN THE PORTRAIT

Untreated portraits exposed to the atmosphere become faded or discolored over time. Such discoloration doesn't happen all at once; it happens gradually as dust and air affect the canvas and the paint. In the same way, the honesty aspect of our character doesn't become faded or discolored all at once. The loss of clarity and "pure color" takes place in small increments related to seemingly small or insignificant choices we make day by day over a long period of time. The chart below lists examples of these seemingly small daily choices that can, over time, discolor your character portrait the same way tiny particles of dirt cause a beautiful painting to lose the color it once had. You may want to review this list to start your thinking about ways dishonesty may have crept into your situation or lifestyle:

DISHONEST PRACTICES SELF-ASSESSMENT

HAVE HAVE NOT

☐ ☐ Conducted personal business on company time

☐ ☐ Failed to admit a mistake and correct it

☐ ☐ Failed to pay suppliers on agreed-to terms as a way to manage cash flow

☐ ☐ Padded resumes and job applications

☐ ☐ Lied in job interviews, either as an applicant or an interviewer

☐ ☐ Advertised my product or service falsely

☐ ☐ Used different prices for different customers (The Bible calls this using different weights and measures. Legitimate reasons for different pricing include cash discounts, volume discounts, scheduling differences in peak seasons, bartering products or services, etc.)

❏ ❏   Padded an expense account

❏ ❏   Padded time sheets

❏ ❏   Lied about attending off-site meetings or trade shows at the company's expense

❏ ❏   Stolen others' words or ideas/not given credit where it's due

❏ ❏   Called in sick when I wasn't

❏ ❏   Written or forwarded dishonest e-mails

❏ ❏   Told "white lies" or used flattery to get ahead

❏ ❏   Padded quality or performance sheets for work not done or verified

❏ ❏   Taken company supplies or resources for personal use

❏ ❏   Accepted an inappropriate gift, gratuity, trip, or favor

❏ ❏   Taken longer breaks and lunch hours than allowed

❏ ❏   Attempted to take extra vacation days I didn't earn

❏ ❏   Used information learned from "inside" sources to trade stocks

❏ ❏   Participated in questionable accounting practices

❏ ❏   Cheated on income tax returns

❏ ❏   Been unfaithful to marriage vows and disloyal to marriage partner

❏ ❏   Broken commitments to friends, family, coworkers, others

❏ ❏   Engaged in negative gossip or spread rumors about someone

❏ ❏   Passed on information someone shared with me in confidence

❏ ❏   Lied

The nearest to perfection that most people ever come is when filling out a job application. —UNKNOWN

After someone reads through a list of biblical standards such as those in the chart on the previous page, a common reaction is to dismiss some of these as "little things." A friend of mine had a habit of lying frequently, usually for no other reason than to make himself look important to women he was dating. When we had become close enough friends that I felt free to call his hand on the habit, he explained this way: "Look, it doesn't hurt anything. They're just little exaggerations. I wouldn't lie about anything important."

I saw things differently. If he lied for "little" reasons, consider how easy it would be to lie when the pressure grew stronger—when he might be about to lose his job or a client, for example. Here's the overriding biblical perspective on the honesty issue: "Whoever can be trusted with very little can also be trusted with much, and whoever is dishonest with very little will also be dishonest with much" (Luke 16:10). Over time, my friend came to see the issue differently.

We need always to be checking for any moisture or chemicals or dust particles in the air that might discolor our character portrait.

The practice of honesty is more convincing than the profession of holiness. —UNKNOWN

The Lord detests lying lips, but he delights in men who are truthful. —PROVERBS 12:22

DIFFERENT STROKES FOR DIFFERENT FOLKS?

Have you ever made that comment? People tend to use it fairly frequently to indicate—somewhat nonjudgmentally—that individuals act differently in the same situations. We may like to chant, "Different strokes for different folks," not realizing that when we do, we may be rationalizing various behaviors to explain why our "different strokes" are not wrong—or even all that different. Here are the most common rationalizations about why we do or don't do certain things:

- "Everyone else does it—even the boss."
- "Nobody cares."
- "Nobody will find out."
- "They figure this kind of loss into the price of the product."
- "It's a silly rule."
- "They don't pay me enough."
- "I don't have time to do it right."
- "It's just a little thing."
- "If they didn't want us to do it, they'd put some safeguards in place, right?"
- "It's not my place to say anything."
- "If I say anything, I'll have everybody angry at me."
- "What do they expect? Surely they must already know this kind of thing goes on."
- "They wouldn't do anything about it anyway."
- "There's no law against it. It's perfectly legal."
- "The guidelines don't make any sense."
- "They deserve this treatment—look what they did to me."

In contrast to these statements, Exodus 23:2 says, "Do not follow the crowd in doing wrong." Sound familiar? Rationalizations don't make wrongs right. But they do underscore the difficulty of specific situations.

I remember a discussion that centered around whether to keep money a client had paid us for work we never did through no fault of our own. Toward the end of the year one of our clients for business-writing workshops called to say she had extra budget money left in the fourth quarter. She wanted us to invoice in December for training she planned to schedule in January. So we billed her as requested. She paid the invoice but never called to schedule the training.

When we called the following March to remind her, we discovered that she'd left the organization and her replacement knew nothing of the pending work. Shocked that our account executive had even told her about the unscheduled work for which we'd been paid, the new person in the job thanked us for our honesty, saying she'd "check around" to find out who in the organization might have requested the training and she would call us back to schedule the classes. When she didn't return the call, we discovered that she also had left the organization.

Again we could find no one who knew anything about the money or seemed interested in scheduling any training amidst their upcoming merger and restructuring. Another year passed and we still hadn't done the work, so with much angst at making a big dent in the year's operating budget, we wrote the chief financial officer, explaining the situation and returning the money.

I tried hard to rationalize about keeping the money "until they called us." After all, we'd done our best to schedule the training, knowing that anybody who knew anything about the situa-

tion had long since left the organization. I even had visions of
a happy ending—like the stories you hear on the news when a
child finds and returns a lost wallet and the owner rewards him
with a new bike for his honesty and trouble. We hoped when
the organization finally hired a new internal training staff, they
would reward us with a big contract. But when our check arrived
at the client's office, what we did get was a callback and an aston-
ished thank-you from the CFO. End of story.

Honesty doesn't always pay—in hard cash, that is. Fortunately, there are more important currencies, such as the knowledge that you did the right thing. Rationalizing would have been
easy, but it would have felt wrong.

> *He is rich or poor according to what he is, not according*
> *to what he has.*   —HENRY WARD BEECHER

THE COLOR CHART: GUIDES FOR HONESTY

Artists don't always select the best color on the first try. Sometimes they have to play with the color to get it just right—the
exact skin tone of the blushing bride, the pasty, pale complexion
of the malnourished child, or the sun-scorched arms of the
soldier. God certainly knew we'd have difficulty with the shades
of gray surrounding issues of honesty, so he gave us a guide—
the Bible—so we wouldn't have to guess.

Yet guess is what many people do. Almost three-quarters of
adults (74 percent) surveyed in a September 2001 poll conducted

by Barna Research said they are concerned about the moral condition of the nation. But when respondents were asked the basis for their moral choices, nearly half (44 percent) said they do whatever will bring them the most pleasing or satisfying results. Roughly one-sixth (17 percent) base moral choices on what they believe will make other people happy or will minimize interpersonal conflict. Only about one-fourth (24 percent) base their moral decisions on religious principles or Bible content. In a separate survey done five years earlier (1997), 35 percent of Christians and 57 percent of non-Christians said that to "get by in life these days, you have to bend the rules a little for your own benefit." Clearly, people do not see the Bible as their guide for honesty. They see shades of gray.

For society as a whole, many of our laws are based on biblical principles. For what the Bible and the law don't address, we typically have organizational policies, procedures, or mission statements to provide guidelines. Additionally, if those things don't address the issue, we have our conscience to guide us.

The tricky thing is that conscience isn't always a trustworthy guide because we can appease it. Suppose we say to someone who wants to lose weight, "Just take this diet pill, and then you can eat as much as you want and still lose weight." Person A, who weighs 110 pounds and normally consumes twelve hundred calories a day, may not "want" more than eight hundred calories a day. But Person B, who weighs 280 pounds and normally consumes four thousand calories a day, *may not* "eat as much as he wants" and still lose weight. His "wanter" has been calibrated to a higher level.

Likewise, some people's conscience has been calibrated to a higher "tolerance" level of what's right and wrong. Some serial killers have convinced themselves that they're doing good by ridding society of other harmful people. Two "consenting adults" may convince themselves that they aren't hurting anyone by their extramarital sexual activity. Students may consider cheating on an exam merely a means to an end—the high grades necessary to gain acceptance into a prestigious university. Conscience alone isn't enough. So rather than depending solely on the conscience test, let's start at the top of the line with the color chart God provided:

- The Bible
- The laws of the land
- Policies, guidelines, procedures, official statements of your organization
- Your conscience

> Do what is right and good in the Lord's sight, so that it may go well with you.   —DEUTERONOMY 6:18

CLEANING THE BRUSHES: FILTER QUESTIONS

Sometimes after consulting all of the above guides, you may still be puzzled because some issues are not really a matter of explicitly stated biblical principles, organizational rules, or governing laws. They really are gray areas. Here are some examples:

- Should you recommend friends for a job when you know they need one but you have serious questions about their skills in the specific area for which they're being considered?
- Should you refuse to give a reference—either positive

or negative—because that's your company's policy when a prospective employer calls to check references?

- Is it right to compliment vain people on their achievements in order to predispose them toward making an appointment with your colleague to hear about your products?

- Is it right to flirt (if you're unmarried and the other person is unmarried) with someone of the opposite sex to predispose that person toward buying a product from you?

- Is it right not to offer training and career advice to an assistant with high potential because you don't want to lose that person if he or she gets a promotion?

- Is it right to have your organization pay for your registration and travel to an industry meeting and then spend part of your time there networking to find another job?

- Is it right to keep quiet about product weaknesses when talking to potential customers if you know those weaknesses may have serious impact for the customers' organization? Should you volunteer negative information if a customer doesn't ask?

In matters of principle, stand like a rock; in matters of taste, swim with the current.   —THOMAS JEFFERSON

When these surface in your situation, you might find it helpful to have some additional screening questions to use in keeping the brushes clean. You might want to ask:

- What does the Bible say?
- Is this action legal?
- Does it follow the stated rules and guidelines of our organization?

- Does this action, inaction, or decision match our stated commitments and advertisements?
- Does it violate values commonly accepted by the community?
- Do I feel comfortable and "at peace" with this decision or action?
- Would I feel embarrassed if my family and friends knew about this?
- Would I be okay if roles were reversed—if someone else were doing or not doing this to me?

> *The one thing that doesn't abide majority rule is a person's conscience.*   —HARPER LEE

CLEANING THE PALETTE COMPLETELY

Artists also occasionally have to clean their palettes to keep colors pure. Although it may seem wasteful to toss out those little dabs of paint, that's preferable to ruining a month's work by brushing on what you thought was pure blue only to discover you've streaked a masterpiece with purple because old, leftover paint had contaminated the fresh paint you squeezed onto the palette. When we're working on our character portrait, we want to be sure that there are no "leftover pigments" that will mar the beauty and purity of the final product. Here are some palette-cleaning techniques.

Confessing a Lie and Setting the Record Straight

Don't delay. Generally, the longer you wait for the "right time" to clean up the problem, the worse the problem becomes. Other people base decisions on wrong information. And more negative consequences are avoided when truth does prevail. There will never be a "good time," so just do it:

1. *Confess:* "I gave you wrong information earlier when I told you that . . ." "I misled you last week when I said that . . ." "It wasn't an accurate assessment of the situation when I said . . ." "I was untruthful yesterday when I said . . ."

2. *Set the record straight:* "The truth is . . ." "The honest situation is that . . ." "A more accurate assessment is . . ."

3. *Apologize and state your feelings about the difficulty you've caused:* "I'm sorry that I didn't tell the complete truth about what happened and for the difficult situation I've put you in. I'm worried that you're going to think less of me, or be disappointed in me, or feel that you can't trust me in the future."

4. *Offer to make restitution:* "I want to do whatever I can to make amends. I think I can . . ." "Here's the least I can do . . ."

The other person may be angry and may "lecture" you about the situation or may even downplay it, saying it is "no big deal." But in either case, you win. If people lecture you, they're probably investing time in you to make sure it doesn't happen again—a good sign they're planning to trust you again. If they downplay it, they're offering you support openly.

> *He who walks in integrity walks securely, but he who perverts his ways will be found out.* —PROVERBS 10:9, NASB

Reporting a Wrong to the Proper Authority

Speaking up about dishonesty happening around you—or worse, dishonesty in which you're expected to participate—can take even more courage. If the authority figure doesn't agree with you and chooses to be an accomplice in the situation, you are not only jeopardizing your own job but also the jobs of others.

Someone once said that "following the path of least resistance is what makes rivers and men crooked." The first step in addressing the issue of dishonesty is to express your conviction in a nonjudgmental way to your direct supervisor:

1. Express your concern with "I" statements: "I don't feel right about doing X." "I have some concerns about X." "I'm uncomfortable about X because it seems to me that . . ."

2. Propose an alternative: "I think a better way to handle this might be . . ." "Couldn't we accomplish the same thing by just doing X?" "I think you and I should contact our VP and let her know that our suppliers are doing X. What do you think?"

3. If nothing changes after talking with your direct supervisor, go to a higher authority. If that person doesn't agree with you or tries to force you to participate, seek a still-higher authority inside or outside the organization and express your concerns.

The only thing necessary for the triumph of evil is for good men to do nothing.
                                                    —EDMUND BURKE

Stealing and Making Things Right

In part 3 of the book we'll talk about a lack of productivity as a form of stealing—that is, not putting in an honest day's work for an honest day's pay. But the self-assessment checklist here

mentions other forms of stealing—taking supplies or money,
padding time sheets or expense accounts, copying software, and
so forth. If you have fallen into these or other practices, try the
following steps to correct such a situation:

1. *Confess:* "I'd like to tell you about a situation I'm not
   proud of." "I've done/been doing something that's gotten
   out of hand and has become a habit. It has been bothering
   me, and I'd like to tell you about it. You may find it
   necessary to dismiss me, and I understand that, but I'd
   like to tell you about it anyway." Then explain the
   situation.

2. *Apologize:* Express your regret for the situation, and state
   how you feel about your part in it: "I'm sorry for the situation, and I know it's wrong because . . ." (Do not justify,
   excuse, or rationalize what you've done.) "I know this
   has cost us a lot of money." "I know some very serious
   decisions have already been made because of this situation
   and they can't be undone." "I know we've lost some
   customers because of this." "I know this makes the whole
   department look bad." "I'm afraid that you're very disappointed in me/angry with me." "I'm worried that you'll
   feel as though you can never put me in a responsible
   position again." "I hope you won't feel as though you
   can't delegate other important projects to me."

3. *Make restitution:* "Here's what I plan to do to try to make
   things right. . . ."

This kind of action requires courage. Be prepared to accept
the consequences of such a confession. But you may also be

surprised and grateful to experience forgiveness. Regardless of the reaction, you will have regained your self-respect—and that's a huge gain.

> *Rather fail with honor than succeed by fraud.*   —SOPHOCLES

> *Sooner or later everyone sits down to a banquet of consequences.*   —ROBERT LOUIS STEVENSON

Adding the Finishing Touches to Your Portrait

When doing a self-assessment of personal honesty, consider God's standards, not those of your next-door neighbors, coworkers, or cousins. That way, when you're ready to paint honesty into your portrait, your brushes and palette will be clean. You'll be able to stay away from gray and paint instead the crisp, clean lines of habit that harden into character.

> *Live in such a way that you would not be ashamed to sell your parrot to the town gossip.*   —WILL ROGERS

> *Nearly all men can stand adversity, but if you want to test a man's character, give him power.*   —ABRAHAM LINCOLN

> *I would have you learn this great fact: that a life of doing right is the wisest life there is. If you live that kind of life, you'll not limp or stumble as you run.*   —PROVERBS 4:11-12, TLB

My worth to God in public is what I am in private.

—OSWALD CHAMBERS

Honesty is the first chapter in the book of wisdom.

—THOMAS JEFFERSON

A reputation once broken may possibly be repaired, but the world will always keep their eyes on the spot where the crack was.

—JOSEPH HALL

TWO

WISDOM

Developing an Artist's Eye for Detail, Damage, and Direction

*A*re you decisive, or do you often second-guess yourself and
agonize over decisions until opportunities are gone?

*D*o others ask your opinion because of your reputation
for giving wise advice?

*D*o you consider yourself wise?

*A*re your insights and decisions a source of pride to you?

BEFORE beginning work on a fresh canvas, artists often take
a photograph of the subject they intend to paint and prop it
under a bright light to study it. They focus for hours on one tiny
section and analyze the detail—the shape of the eye, the exact
color of the iris, the length of the lashes, the arch of the eyebrow,
the bridge of the nose, the broken vein in the eyelid, the tiny scar
near the outside corner, the crow's feet that spread to the edges
of the cheeks. After they analyze, then they create.

So it is with wise people in every walk of life. They focus, analyze, and study a situation. After they assess, then they decide and act. With that in mind, consider the following scenarios:

Scenario 1.

An employee has worked for your small business for many years. When he came from another industry, he had no previous experience in the field. You train him in all aspects of the job and give him proprietary information about technologies, pricing, and clients. At his request and due to a change in his personal situation, he asks to switch from full-time-employee status to contractor status. You agree to the change and continue to use his services on that basis. After several more years he terminates his relationship as contractor in order to compete with you. He refuses all requests to let your representative review his newly developed materials for possible copyright infringement of your concepts or techniques. Rather than develop his own client base among a huge universe of prospects, he contacts those specific individuals with whom you have paid him to develop a relationship while he worked for you and tries to sell them competing services.

Dilemma: How do you handle the situation?

Scenario 2.

A new employee is assigned to your work team. She's pleasant, friendly, supportive, and has a great sense of humor that the team enjoys. But she does not pull her weight on key projects. You've noticed that her work is far inferior to that of the rest of the group, and the team continues to be penalized and loses bonuses during the quarterly quality-review process because of her errors. Although she has apologized profusely, as your team moves into more difficult assignments, you can see that your colleague simply does not have the skills to handle the job. She has been offered training but has been unable to improve her skills. In fact, she has confided to you that she doesn't feel competent to handle the job but really needs the money and is afraid she can't find a position elsewhere at her age and without a formal education. Your manager has asked your opinion of her work and what you think should be done.

Dilemma: How would you handle the situation?

Scenario 3.
A family in need approaches your church group for help. The group members contribute generously toward the family's immediate needs so that they can buy clothes, food, and medicine. Then the father attends another church, again asking for help. When you offer to go with him to the mall to buy clothes, he is less interested in the help. A little investigation turns up this additional information: He has visited almost every adult group in your church, asking for donations to help his wife. His depressed wife and their two adult sons live in a two-bedroom apartment. The church has already made arrangements to pay for their medicine each month—the pharmacy bills the church directly. But the husband has had repeated run-ins with the pharmacy staff because of his attempts to add candy, sodas, and gifts to the medicine bills. Neither of the adult sons works. The man's wife is sick and depressed, but she wants no visits from church members.

Dilemma: What should you do in this situation?

Scenario 4.

Your twenty-one-year-old daughter, just one semester short of having her degree in chemistry, calls to say she's dropping out of college. She says she met an entrepreneur with a product that will revolutionize the way carpet cleaning is done. She plans to become his research scientist and begin work on new cleaning formulas. She says that her salary is "minimal" now but assures you that she's going to get a piece of the action when the company goes public "sometime in the next year or two."

Dilemma: How do you handle the situation?

Scenario 5.

A client calls to book consulting time for September 15–17. You agree on the dates, prepare for the project, and turn down other business on those dates. A week before the consulting project is to begin, you notice that you still have not received the client's first half of the deposit for the work, as the contract stipulates. You phone the client to make sure that everything is still a "go." He mentions the hurricane and flooding in their area in the past two weeks, during which many have been out of the office, but assures you that the check is "in process." Since you've worked for the client at other locations on many occasions, you act in good faith and travel to the client's site.

The next morning the client phones your hotel to say he has decided to cancel the project because of the low quarterly earnings report just posted. He refuses to pay for the contracted engagement after his last-minute cancellation despite the fact that you've already completed work in preparation for the meeting and have turned down other engagements for these dates. According to the contract, he owes you the full fee. Other directors and

partners in the firm have been honest in their dealings; this
individual has not. You value the long-term relationship, yet
this situation has cost you a good deal of money.

Dilemma: What position should you take on this deal?

Wisdom consists of the anticipation of consequences.

—NORMAN COUSINS

*Wisdom does not consist so much in knowing what to do,
as in knowing what not to do when you are ignorant; the
chief fault of the unwise is driving toward conclusions from
insufficient premises.* —SYDNEY HARRIS

You may face situations and decisions similar to these every
day: business dealings, financial setbacks, career choices, problems with children, conflicts with in-laws, ethical—if not legal—
issues with coworkers, employees, bosses, neighbors, or the
community. To handle many of them requires the patience
of Job, the wisdom of Solomon, and the love of Jesus.

It is never wise to be cocksure.   —OSWALD CHAMBERS

*It does not take much strength to do things, but it requires
great strength to decide what to do.*   —ELBERT HUBBARD

WHO'S THE WISE GUY—OR GAL?
We say people are knowledgeable if they have information, facts,
or skills. A very knowledgeable person may even show mastery
of a craft, a job, or a topic.

In contrast, wisdom refers to superior mental capabilities in *applying* knowledge and skill in a specific situation at the right time, in the right way, for a specific purpose, for the best outcome, for all concerned.

> *Knowledge leads us from the simple to the complex; wisdom leads us from the complex to the simple.* —UNKNOWN

> *Knowledge comes by taking things apart: analysis. But wisdom comes by putting things together.*
>
> —JOHN A. MORRISON

In the Bible, wisdom is also used to describe superior mental capabilities that involve a *moral aspect*—the ability to understand and do good (see 2 Kings 2:1-6; 1 Kings 3:16-28; and Deuteronomy 1:13). A relationship with God and knowledge of his character are the foundation for this kind of wisdom: "The fear of the Lord is the beginning of wisdom" (Proverbs 9:10 and Psalm 111:10).

Decisiveness—evaluating courses of action quickly and accurately—comes from such wisdom. Organization and efficiency enter the picture as you use your resources—money, people, equipment, buildings, technology, food, supplies, data, information, or whatever—in the most effective way to accomplish your mission with the most moral outcome in mind.

The Greek philosopher Plato (ca. 428–347 B.C.) defined wisdom as having four parts: (1) doing things right, (2) living consistently—in public and private, (3) living courageously and meeting danger head-on, and (4) living a disciplined life of moderation. There's nothing to argue about there—except that Plato left God out of the equation as the basis for moral living.

We all want to be wise. And most of us recognize wisdom when we hear it, but we sometimes have difficulty developing it into our own character portrait from the beginning because wisdom grows slowly over time. For that reason, it's helpful to have a sense of the characteristics of wisdom so that we will know what we're aiming for as we work on that aspect of our character portrait.

> *The person who knows "how" will always have a job. The person who knows "why" will always be his boss.*
> —DIANE RAVITCH

> *An ounce of application is worth a ton of abstraction.*
> —BOOKER T. WASHINGTON

THE COLOR AND CANDOR OF WISDOM

How can we begin to sketch in the color of wisdom on our portraits? Let's consider the biblical characteristics of wisdom on the canvas. Those who have wisdom

- hold their tongues; think before speaking (see Proverbs 10:19; 21:23; 29:11)
- seek advice from many counselors (see Proverbs 13:10; 19:20)
- listen with an open mind and weigh facts and ideas before

deciding whether to accept or reject them as valid (see
Proverbs 3:5; 18:13)
- accept feedback and correction (see Proverbs 15:31-32;
  10:8)
- learn continually (see Proverbs 1:5)
- spend their time carefully, are organized, and prioritize
  tasks (see Proverbs 24:27, 33-34; 31:27; Colossians 4:5)
- think strategically and plan ahead (see Proverbs 6:6-8;
  21:20; 24:27; 27:23-24; 31:15-18, 21)
- live a disciplined, prudent, moderate lifestyle (see Proverbs
  1:3; 25:28)
- show discretion, know how to tell right from wrong,
  and choose accordingly (see Proverbs 1:4; 2:11)
- hang out with other wise people (see Proverbs 13:20)
- are humble (see Proverbs 8:13; 13:10; 22:4; 25:6; 26:12;
  27:2; 29:3)

A wise man has great power.   —PROVERBS 24:5

Wisdom is supreme; . . . though it cost all you have, get
understanding.   —PROVERBS 4:7

Sometimes it's easier to understand a concept by focusing on
what it is not, by looking at its opposite. If we say that the opposite of wisdom is foolishness, then in this case, we can say that
those who exhibit foolishness:

- speak without thinking
- do it "my way" without asking advice from others
- make up their minds before hearing all sides of an issue
  or having all the facts

- decide things without determining the proper criteria for a decision
- become defensive when receiving negative feedback and refuse corrective instruction
- think they know all there is about a subject, person, or situation and refuse to learn more
- waste time and persist in being disorganized
- become impatient when waiting for God to act on their behalf
- refuse to plan ahead; have no goals
- live an undisciplined life and give in to all their passions and desires, doing what they want when they want, regardless of who gets hurt
- show no regard for what's right or wrong in any given situation—whether related to words, actions, or attitudes
- hang out with other foolish people who lead them to do unwise things
- are arrogant and oblivious to their need to change

Not a pretty picture, is it? You don't find these character portraits in the best art galleries.

Many receive advice; only the wise profit by it.

—PUBLILIUS SYRUS

Wise men change their minds, fools never.

—ENGLISH PROVERB

The doorstep to the temple of wisdom is a knowledge of our own ignorance.   —CHARLES HADDON SPURGEON

"BLUE RIBBONS" IN THE ART GALLERY

What can you expect from living a wise life? What might others notice and comment on if they were strolling through an art gallery containing portraits of the wisest people? Here are the rewards of wisdom promised in the the book of Proverbs:

Honor and a Good Reputation (Proverbs 3:4, 35; 8:18): You will become known for your wise decisions. People will seek you out for advice. Others will recognize and honor the achievements you have gained by having superior wisdom.

Fidelity in Marriage (Proverbs 5:15-20; 2:16): Your wisdom will lead you to safeguard your marriage by honoring your marriage vows. Wisdom will give you strength to overcome sexual temptations that cause weaker persons to fall. Not only will you be faithful in sexual ways, but you will cherish your spouse, showing loyalty and honor to that person whether he or she is present or not. A bond of mutual respect and honor will develop between you and all those who observe your marriage relationship.

Safety (Proverbs 1:33; 3:23; 4:6; 28:18; 29:5): Wisdom will lead you to an awareness of dangers and traps, whether physical, financial, or spiritual. When you must go into harm's way, God-given wisdom will give you cunning and skill and the attitude (desire) to escape.

Prosperity (Proverbs 3:2, 16; 8:18, 21): Having wisdom will cause you to prosper in many ways—sometimes with wealth, sometimes with health, sometimes with loving family and friends, sometimes with opportunities.

Long Life (Proverbs 3:1-2, 16): Wisdom will lead us to a lifestyle that promotes long life. Practicing discipline and moderation in diet, exercise, and rest contributes to good health, energy, and productivity.

Blessedness (Proverbs 8:32, 34): Wisdom leads to God's favor and approval. If you act in wise ways, God will show you his favor and use you to accomplish his work in the world.

Knowledge of God (Proverbs 2:5; 3:5-6): We learn how to make better everyday decisions as we know and understand more about God's own character and teachings.

Quite an impressive list, isn't it! Other rewards—a gold watch at retirement, a promotion to CEO, a trip for two to Hawaii, a new home in the heights, things that some people work a lifetime to attain—pale in comparison with these lasting rewards.

If you read through this list and see that you're not experiencing all of these benefits, does it mean you're unwise? Not necessarily. If someone dies in a car accident at age thirty-two without experiencing the "long life" mentioned in the list above, does that mean he or she was not wise? Not necessarily.

These are *general principles* about the benefits of wisdom; they are not necessarily promises about the way our lives will turn out if we follow them. Because God sometimes permits sin and its consequences to intervene in our lives, individually we may not experience some of these benefits until eternity. But certainly a life lived according to God's wisdom still brings rewards as we live it day by day.

> *Wise are they who have learned these truths: Trouble is temporary. Time is a tonic. Tribulation is a test tube.*
>
> —UNKNOWN

WHAT'S THE FIRST BRUSHSTROKE ON WISDOM?

Where do you look for wisdom? Some people check their horoscope, read tea leaves, ask astrologers, search the Internet, chant and hum, and investigate religious writings from all over the world, all in the effort to find the source of true wisdom. If you want real wisdom, you have to look in the right place: wisdom comes from God. Proverbs 2:6 says, "The Lord gives wisdom, and from his mouth come knowledge and understanding."

What do you have to do to get that wisdom? Ask: "If any of you lacks wisdom, he should ask God, who gives generously to all without finding fault, and it will be given to him," says James 1:5. Sounds pretty straightforward, doesn't it? There are some stipulations stated elsewhere, particularly in Proverbs 2. So here, in a nutshell, is the process for gaining wisdom.

Ask from the Right Source

God is the beginning of wisdom—the foundation, the moral basis upon which everything else rests. But that's no excuse to plead ignorance about every other subject. God gave us our mental faculties to use in discovering the world around us—art, science, math, languages, history, etc. The more knowledge and understanding we gain, the better our glimpse into the richness and vastness of the universe God created for us to explore. Some of us are blessed with special insights, some with knowledge, some with common sense, some with specific skills and talents, some with intuition.

In fact, in 1983 Howard Gardner expanded the concept of intelligence when he proposed his Theory of Multiple Intelligences, which is rapidly being incorporated into our culture and school curricula. He suggested that people are generally "smart" in one or more of seven ways: logical-mathematical intelligence, linguistic intelligence, spatial intelligence, musical intelligence, bodily kinesthetic intelligence, interpersonal intelligence, and intrapersonal intelligence. For example, some people have a stronger aptitude for understanding mathematical concepts; others are more musically inclined; still others have a special sense in reading people.

Whatever the intelligence, God is the source of all these capacities. We know and learn in each of these ways because that's the way he created us.

Commit to Right Choices and Avoid Moral Pitfalls

When there are new recruits in the workplace, most people are committed to helping them learn the job. As long as these new employees come to work on time, pay attention to instructions, show up for meetings, and take care of assigned equipment, you assume they're committed to the job and you're willing to make the effort to teach them the ropes. But you lose patience if it becomes obvious that the new hires have no commitment to the job—if they call in sick repeatedly, fail to return phone calls, mistreat equipment, ignore instructions, and disregard company policy.

In the same way, God says he reveals wisdom only to those who show a commitment to make morally right choices. He will not waste his resources on those who continue to live and act irresponsibly with the insights he provides. That's not to say you won't make bad decisions from time to time, which brings us to the next point.

Learn from Your Mistakes

You may make mistakes, but you're not characterized by them. If you're wise, you'll train yourself to identify what went wrong so that you can grow from the experience and avoid making the same mistake the next time around: Those who are "mature . . .

have trained themselves to recognize the difference between right and wrong and then do what is right" (Hebrews 5:14, NLT). If at first you don't succeed, as the old saying goes, try, try again. If you still don't succeed, stop, sit down, and think it over. Persistence is a noble virtue, but it's no substitute for analysis.

> *Wisdom is seldom gained without suffering.*
>
> —SIR ARTHUR HELPS

Search for Wisdom Enthusiastically, Persistently, and Continually

You'll never arrive at the end of your wisdom education and pronounce yourself a mature, wise person. You don't go online, order it through a mouse click, charge it to your credit card, and download it while you have dinner. God said the journey to wisdom requires day-to-day effort to evaluate and gain insight, time to pray and seek advice, commitment to make hard choices, and persistence to follow through on decisions: "Listen to me and treasure my instructions. Tune your ears to wisdom, and concentrate on understanding. Cry out for insight and understanding. Search for them as you would for lost money or hidden treasure. Then you will understand what it means to fear the Lord, and you will gain knowledge of God" (Proverbs 2:1-5, NLT). If you're willing to make the trip, God will act as your guide.

> *How much better to get wisdom than gold, to choose understanding rather than silver!*   —PROVERBS 16:16

> *A prudent question is one-half of wisdom.*   —FRANCIS BACON

Adding the Finishing Touches to Your Portrait

The benefits of wisdom certainly whet the appetite. If you don't see many of the payoffs of wisdom in your life right now, put the picture under a brighter light. Have you lost focus on the details?

If you often second-guess yourself on decisions, take another look at the characteristics of the wise person to discover steps you may be missing in the decision-making process: Are you committed up front to doing the morally right thing—whatever you ultimately determine that to be in any specific situation? Are you asking advice from the right people? Is a lack of analysis, strategic thinking, and planning ahead forcing you to make decisions in the moment of crisis?

If, on the other hand, others routinely ask your opinions about their important decisions, chances are that they have begun to recognize wisdom in you, and your responsibility will grow even greater as you advise them.

Add the finishing touches, pause to reflect and evaluate, but never stop painting.

> *Colors fade, temples crumble, empires fall, but wise words endure.*
> —EDWARD L. THORNDIKE

> *Wisdom is the quality that keeps you from getting into situations where you need it.*
> —DOUG LARSON

> *More gold has been mined from the thoughts of men than has ever been taken from the earth.*
> —NAPOLEON HILL

Where the river is deepest, it makes the least noise.

—ITALIAN PROVERB

Trust in the Lord with all your heart and lean not on your own understanding.   —PROVERBS 3:5

For the value of wisdom is far above rubies; nothing can be compared with it.   —PROVERBS 8:11, TLB

Discernment is God's call to intercession, never to faultfinding.

—CORRIE TEN BOOM

THREE

DETERMINATION
Studying the Landscape to Get from Here to There

𝒟o you struggle with change or welcome it?

𝒜re you a person of action, or would you categorize
yourself as a "wait and see" type?

𝒟o you have goals in every area of life—personal-growth goals,
work goals, family goals, financial goals, spiritual goals?

𝒟o others consider you a responsible person?

ROGER CRAWFORD has only one leg and short stubs for arms.
Born with these disabilities, he has had a few struggles in his life.
His preteen daughter describes him to her classmates as the dad
who has a little difficulty opening the peanut-butter jar. Despite
a few dozen other setbacks along the way, Roger became a Divi-
sion I athlete and has been certified by the United States Professional Tennis Association. He is also an accomplished author

and speaker who travels all over the world to encourage others who face adversity. Determination has been the name of his game. Change has been his calling card.

Life consists of revolving doors, unfulfilled promises, broken relationships, unrealized dreams, depressing tragedies, escalating discussions, deepening wounds, tighter policies, faster processes, mounting commitments, missing paperwork, overwhelming information. To think otherwise is self-deception. How do we deal with so much ongoing change? The answer to that question leads us to the next element in our character portrait: determination.

Determination is the act of coming to a fixed realization or conclusion about something. In this particular instance, determination is related to a realization that change may affect any part of your life at any moment and that any present struggle to persevere through that change is simply part of future achievement. Once you've come to that point, you need to decide what you're going to do in the face of that realization. You'll need to make some choices.

> *You will not grow if you sit in a beautiful flower garden,*
> *but you will grow if you are sick, in pain, experience losses,*
> *and if you do not put your head in the sand, but take the*
> *pain and learn to accept it, not as a curse or punishment*
> *but as a gift to you with a very, very specific purpose.*
> —ELIZABETH KUBLER-ROSS

> *Strength and growth come only through continuous effort*
> *and struggle.*   —NAPOLEON HILL

LIFE AS A VICTIM OR A VICTOR?

If you were to pose as a model for an artist painting two portraits, would you choose to pose as a victim or a victor?

In our culture today it has become fashionable to pose as a victim. Criminals shed responsibility for crimes because they were victims of poor parenting or were raised in foster homes. Students shed responsibility for cheating on exams because they are victims of incompetent teachers, inadequate schools, or neglectful parents. Managers shed responsibility for disrespecting their employees because they are victims of uncaring bosses themselves. Mothers drown children because they are victims of spousal abuse. Snipers shoot innocent coworkers because they are victims of a layoff.

I'm painting in broad strokes here; in no way do I mean to minimize the serious problems of parental abuse, spousal abuse, or mental illness. Life from the viewpoint of a victim can only be disheartening. Thinking of yourself as a victim produces despair and hopelessness. Living life with a victim mentality enslaves you—mentally, physically, emotionally, and spiritually. Your goal must be a life of action, not reaction. And the first brush stroke that leads to action is making a commitment to change your viewpoint for the future.

Some people succeed because they are destined to, but most people succeed because they are determined to. —UNKNOWN

Vision is the world's most desperate need. There are no hopeless situations, only people who think hopelessly.

—WINIFRED NEWMAN

FLEXIBILITY IS YOUR ONLY SECURITY

Determination involves being flexible enough to act in whatever circumstances God places you without becoming distracted before completing your mission.

If you want to live *on the edge* of excitement, you have to be flexible enough to go *over the edge* when facing a change in schedules, a change in staff, a change in policy, a change in procedures, a change in culture, a change in goals.

Some people have confused determination with rigidity. Determination does mean persistently driving ahead—but not necessarily on the same road . . . in the same Chevy truck. Those who get rigid by stubbornly sticking to the same ruts and routes will eventually find themselves driving in circles instead of moving ahead.

At seventy-eight, my mom spends time on the Internet every day, communicates with her friends by e-mail, changes her house decorations for every holiday season, and continually tries new recipes for our family gatherings and various parties she hosts at her home. Flexibility has nothing to do with age; it's a mind-set. Like brittle plastic, inflexible people break far too easily. Flexibility prepares you for the future, whatever your future holds.

> *In the race for success, speed is less important than stamina. The sticker outlasts the sprinter in life's race. In America we breed many hares but not so many tortoises.* —B. C. FORBES

> *The main dangers in this life are the people who want to change everything . . . or nothing.* —LADY NANCY ASTOR

ARE YOU IN THE MOOD?

Determination also involves initiative. Initiative to complete important tasks and projects despite obstacles. Initiative to set goals for the future. Initiative for personal growth.

Too much of life—from our menu choices to our music, from our career manager to our marriage partner, from our vacations to our hobbies—rocks along on our moods, our emotional ups and downs:

- "What are you in the **mood** for—Chinese food or Italian?"
- "So where do you **feel** like going for vacation—the Caribbean or home to see your parents?"
- "Did you ask for the new assignment, or are you going to wait until your boss is in a better **mood** after first-quarter earnings are in?"
- "The minute she walked into the room, it **felt** magical, and I **fell in love**."
- "Are you in the **mood** to discuss the money issue, or shall we wait until tomorrow?"

It seems as if sometimes even life-and-death situations turn on our mood swings. So when it comes to the difficult tasks, projects, duties, and commitments in life, it's understandable why people may think they need to rely on their emotions for a jump start.

The common perception is that we need to be motivated *before* we act, but actually the reverse is true—action often precedes motivation. That's certainly the case where exercise is concerned. If I waited until I felt motivated, I'd never work out. So, motivated or not, I force myself to start lifting the weights.

Then once I start exercising and the blood starts pumping, I feel better for the rest of the workout and for hours afterward and I'm motivated to do it again the next time.

"Getting going" or "priming the pump" is often the most difficult part of any task. After you take that first action, you're often set for the entire project. Action compels you into a project—or into a long-term growth process.

> *Keep on going, and the chances are that you will stumble on something, perhaps when you are least expecting it. I never heard of anyone ever stumbling on something sitting down.*
> —CHARLES F. KETTERING

For example, you may have to make yourself enroll in a course and *then* you become motivated to study as you become interested and excited by the topics of discussion, reading materials, and assigned projects. You may make yourself cut up the credit card so that you can no longer buy impulsively on credit. *Then* you get motivated to get all your finances in order, pay off all your bills, and then have money to save and invest. You decide to be more punctual for work, so you set the alarm clock earlier and force yourself to get up. *Then* after you're up, you motivate yourself to stay up and learn to adjust your routine to make the new schedule more appealing and workable.

Whatever the situation, project, or goal, moods are highly unpredictable. So start with activity. Motivation will follow.

> *Life does not tend to reward wishing or dreaming. Never be impressed by what you know. Only be impressed by what you do with what you know.*
> —NANCI McGRAW

I never heard anything about the resolutions of the apostles, but a great deal about their acts.   —HORACE MANN

Rather than focus on the distant future, make your first step what lies directly in front of you—what needs to be done today. Just act. Do something to move ahead. Then set your longer-term goals, and formulate your plans to achieve them.

Yes, I heartily agree in principle with Malcolm Forbes, who said, "If you don't know what you want to do, it's harder to do it." Goals are good. Goals are great. But goals alone never substitute for action. Once you have some momentum, then get a goal. Get a great big auspicious goal. Add deadlines. Goals without deadlines are only wishes. Then lay out your plans. Work your plans. Modify your plans periodically to accommodate significant other plans in your life. Evaluate your progress. Raise or lower the bar accordingly. Then go again. As you do, you will grow.

Obstacles are those frightful things you see when you take your eyes off the goal.   —HANNAH MORE

Too many of us shoot blanks when aiming at our goals.   —UNKNOWN

Ask and it will be given to you; seek and you will find; knock and the door will be opened to you.   —MATTHEW 7:7

More men fail through lack of purpose than through lack of talent.   —BILLY SUNDAY

ACCOUNTABILITY COUNTS AND RESPONSIBILITY IS REASONABLE

Finally, determination involves using everything at your disposal—all your energy and all your resources—to fulfill your commitments or live up to your own and others' reasonable expectations of you. Being a strong, determined person includes being accountable for your actions. Regardless of their good intentions or lack of wrong intentions, strong, determined people accept responsibility for the consequences of their decisions, actions, and inactions.

> *I have long since come to believe that people never mean half of what they say, and that it is best to disregard their talk and judge only their actions.*   —DOROTHY DAY

> *God gives us the ingredients for our daily bread, but he expects us to do the baking.*   —UNKNOWN

We can't turn on the television today or read a magazine without hearing or reading stories or commentaries about deadbeat dads, neglectful mothers, irresponsible teens, irresponsible executives concerned only with short-term profits rather than the long-term health of their organization, irresponsible managers lopping off divisions and departments during mergers, irresponsible medical officials more concerned with profit than with patients, irresponsible consultants making recommendations without adequate study, irresponsible politicians engaged in rhetoric that endangers national security, and irresponsible reporters passing on unsubstantiated claims.

For the past few decades, our society has raised a resound-

ing cry for responsibility. In 1948 the World Council of
Churches adopted a slogan referring to a "responsible society."
In 1994 the Republican Party's "Personal Responsibility Act"
was part of its *Contract with America*. As Os Guinness points
out in his excellent book *The Call*, no discussion of morals
is complete without a reference to this word *responsible*. In
context, we use the word *good* in reference to ethics, *nice* when
referring to our neighbors or fellow citizens, *professional* when
relating in the business world, and *reliable* when talking about
media sources—all of which words are substitutes for the term
responsible.

We live in a time when leaders say that they "take full responsibility" for errors and wrongdoing in their organizations and
insist that "the buck stops" with them while in the next breath
they deny any guilt when things go wrong. In older societies
and smaller communities, visibility kept people accountable.
In today's culture of anonymity, more and more people are
invisible—on the job, in the church, even in our families—than
in any other time in history.

Supervisors may not see what their employees do for months
at a time. Ministers may control church activities and finances
with only rubber-stamp approval by committees or boards not
involved on a daily basis. Spouses may commute from opposite
coasts and rendezvous only on the weekend. Teens may live in
isolation in their rooms, appearing only for school, meals, and
questions about laundry or lunch money.

When leaders in our corporations, our government, and
our megachurches become invisible, their activities lack
accountability. Finding themselves in those places of invisi-
bility can be tempting—as many leaders will attest. Families

whose members feel no accountability disintegrate during difficulty.

The only thing that changes this trend of irresponsibility in today's culture of anonymity are the portraits of those who understand this fact: Ultimate accountability for all of us in all situations is to God. He knows the facts, intentions, causes, costs, and ripples of all our decisions and behavior.

A winner makes commitments; a loser makes promises.

—FANUEL TIJINGAETE

Adding the Finishing Touches to Your Portrait

Beginning artists are exposed to many styles of art: impressionism, realisim, abstract. To discover where their own talents lie, they need to experiment with many art forms and techniques. They try their hand at painting still lifes, detailed portraits, and cartoons and experiment with watercolors, oils, charcoal, and pastels. On the weekends you may find them strolling through art museums, studying the masterpieces of Van Gogh, Rembrandt, or Picasso, but you probably won't hear them blame the masters if their own creations don't turn out as well. To become accomplished artists themselves will require that they set their own goals, take the initiative to practice their technique, and persist until they develop their own style.

The same can be said of any other determined people. They navigate change and remain flexible as they overcome obstacles and distractions. They take the initiative to set goals, act, grow, persist, and be responsible for their action or inaction. Their reputation rests on it.

As you add determination to the final portrait, consider change as inevitable as meals, moods, and Mondays. Don't let yourself feel victimized by change any more than you would feel victimized by finding a new diamond in your backyard or a new decade on your calendar.

Although you do want to take the time to select the appropriate colors, brushes, and techniques for your portrait, delaying too long increases the chance that you'll miss your best opportunities altogether.

If God sent Jesus to earth with a goal rather than just to "while away the time doing good for a few years," you can be sure that goal setting is important. Goals guide you in the right direction. Activity jump-starts your motivation to reach them.

> *A determined soul will do more with a rusty monkey wrench than a loafer will accomplish with all the tools in a machine shop.* —RUPERT HUGHES

> *Weak men wait for opportunities; strong men make them.* —ORISON SWETT MARDEN

> *The difference between perseverance and obstinacy is that one often comes from a strong will, and the other from a strong won't.* —HARRIET WARD BEECHER

> *Genius is perseverance in disguise.* —MIKE NEWLIN

FOUR

COURAGE
Painting in the Dark

$\mathcal{W}$hat do you fear?

$\mathcal{A}$re you courageous when it counts?

$\mathcal{W}$hat's the biggest loss you've risked for your faith?

$\mathcal{H}$ow do you increase your courage?

IN OUR CULTURE, the difference between a "wimp" and a coward is a matter only of degree. Being labeled a coward ranks right up there with being called a liar, a thief, or a cheat. Pop culture tends to focus on the physical aspects of courage, with macho movie heroes portrayed by people like John Wayne, Clint Eastwood, Harrison Ford, Arnold Schwarzenegger, Mel Gibson, Tom Selleck, Chuck Norris, Sylvester Stallone, and Bruce Willis. Although all cultures throughout history have admired physical courage, emotional and moral courage seems to be harder to find in leaders of recent years.

WHAT ARE YOU AFRAID OF?

I'd hate to be a soldier in a fearless general's army, a patient under the knife of a fearless surgeon, or an employee working for a fearless manager. The book of Proverbs calls a fearless person a reckless fool because such people charge ahead instead of considering the consequences before they act (Proverbs 14:16). Someone who has not learned what to fear lacks a solid education.

"Courage is knowing *what* to fear," the Greek philosopher Plato concluded. A healthy respect for danger shows that a person has assessed the situation, the options, and the outcomes. Courage calls for acting, speaking, doing, or standing in the face of fear, despite loss or gain hanging in the balance. Courage is facing fear head-on.

> *Mountain climbers connect themselves to one another with a rope to keep the one at the end from going home.*
> —CHARLES R. SWINDOLL

> *Courage is fear that has said its prayers.*—DOROTHY BERNARD

What's on your list of things that frighten you? My list includes snakes, tornadoes, war, heart attacks, stock-market crashes, the moral decay of our country—and people who aren't afraid of anything. Our lists may differ according to our experiences, but we have one thing in common: the need to act in the face of fear, the need to feel peace and strength to go about our daily lives, and the need to risk loss to do right.

The English word *crisis* is written in Chinese by combining two characters—one meaning "danger" and the other meaning "opportunity." We don't get courage until we need it: courage comes to us in a crisis and creates an opportunity for change. How we react determines whether we'll walk away with growth or with negative consequences.

Unfortunately, we're not always open to opportunity and growth. Risk rankles us. Our entire way of life today seems to be dedicated to getting guarantees. From the cradle to the grave, many people expect to be informed, warned, supported, insulated, and protected from every risk—risks that people in other countries face daily. If something tragic happens, we often expect our government to stand ready with safety nets, crutches, and a checkbook.

This born-and-bred aversion to risk means we have to make a conscious effort to study the fine lines of detail if we intend to paint courage into our character portrait.

Man cannot discover new oceans unless he has the courage to lose sight of the shore.   —UNKNOWN

He who faces no calamity will need no courage.
                                        —HARRY EMERSON FOSDICK

COURAGE IS CAREFUL CHOICES, NOT CRAZY CONFUSION

You've probably heard it said that people fall in love with "reckless abandon" or that they "throw caution to the wind" as they embark on an adventure. That story line may make a great movie, but it's not part of the portrait of a courageous character.

In the Old Testament we find the story of Gideon, who was preparing to fight against the Midianites. He started out with an army of thirty-two thousand soldiers. Then God, not wanting

Israel to be able to boast that they defeated the enemy by their own strength, told Gideon to send home "anyone who trembles with fear"; that is, cowards. So Gideon told those who were afraid to go home. Overnight twenty-two thousand men bailed out. That left Gideon with an army of ten thousand brave soldiers.

But Gideon still wasn't ready to take on the enemy. In addition to the self-assessment on bravery, God told him to check out the remaining soldiers on one other detail: Gideon was to take them down to the river to let them and their animals have a drink—and be very observant during the process. As he watched, he divided the soldiers into two groups: (1) those who laid aside their weapons, bent their heads to the water's edge, and scooped up the water with both hands and (2) those who dipped one hand into the river and brought the water up to their mouth while keeping an eye on their surroundings and one hand free to draw their swords. The second group wasn't difficult to count—it contained only three hundred alert soldiers. Gideon sent the other ninety-seven hundred home. He needed soldiers who were not only courageous but also smart.

God never asks us to do foolhardy things. In fact we presume on God if we expect him to take care of us when we act rashly without forethought, prayer, and guidance. Courage is not jumping off a cliff and then searching for the safety net on the way down.

DREAMS MAY DEMAND COURAGE

We typically think of courage coupled with adversity. But occasionally courage keeps company with self-doubt. You may feel called to move across country where you will have no family to lend support, to try your hand at writing the next big box-office hit, or to give up a secure paycheck and move to the other side of the world to teach English and dispense food in a tiny farming village.

James Bryant Conant, former president of Harvard University, pointed out in *Success* magazine, "Behold the turtle: He only makes progress when he sticks his neck out." You may have everything to gain from acting courageously, but that doesn't mean you may not fear taking risks. Moving ahead along uncharted paths and facing tough decisions is . . . well, . . . risky.

Sharing your dreams forces you to ratchet the courage up a notch because once you have told someone else about them, you become accountable to that person. Dreams unshared may fade into oblivion. Dreams declared demand defense and dare you to act boldly.

> *America was not built on fear. America was built on courage, on imagination, and unbeatable determination to do the job at hand.*   —HARRY S. TRUMAN

COURAGE RISKS LOSS FOR WHAT'S RIGHT

In the Old Testament, Hebrew midwives risked their lives when they disobeyed the Pharaoh's order to kill male children under the age of two. Joseph risked his job in the palace and ended up in prison unjustly when he chose to refuse the advances of Potiphar's wife rather than betray his friend and boss Potiphar.

Living with courage may demand that you report unethical activities at your workplace to the authorities. It may mean resigning your job if a superior asks you to participate in something immoral or unethical. It may mean being passed over for promotion because you refuse to steal credit for someone else's ideas or work. As someone once said, "You have to choose the foxhole you're willing to die in."

Courage may mean losing a friendship because you considered it more important to talk straight to your neighbors about their wayward teen's criminal behavior than to let the parents discover it on their own. Living with courage may mean making a momentarily unpopular management decision for the long-term health of the organization and the overall benefit of the group. It may mean becoming politically active in a school or community in your sphere of influence.

The common denominator in all these examples is that the bigger the loss you risk and the higher the likelihood of failure, the greater the courage required.

> There are risks and costs to action. But they are far less than the long range risks of comfortable inaction.
>
> —JOHN F. KENNEDY

COURAGE CONVICTS

We often hear of leaders who speak up or lead others with the "courage of their convictions." As author Sydney J. Harris pointed out, "Nero, Caligula, Attila, and Hitler all had the courage of their convictions—but not one had the courage to *examine* his convictions, or to change them. That may be the real test of character—the ability to admit mistakes in front of a group, to change your mind, to say, 'I was wrong.'"

Courage demands that we confront our own beliefs,

actions, shortcomings, and inconsistencies as well as those of others. Sometimes we need to hear the still, small voice in our head. Sometimes it is the shout or the calm voice of reason from our spouse, our teen, or an enemy who calls us to confront our inconsistencies, admit our mistakes, or change our ways.

Cowards bluff and press on despite the consequences. The courageous confess errors in judgment and correct their course.

> *Courage is what it takes to stand up and speak; courage is also what it takes to sit down and listen.*
> —WINSTON CHURCHILL

COURAGE CAN BE CREATIVE

I've never been one to tell the dentist to drill without first deadening the nerve. Some people manage to think creatively and live courageously enough to find the loopholes in life's pain. In a tough situation, nobody says that you have to drive straight into the center of the storm. Thinking creatively about how to accomplish your goal may be both smart and courageous.

Robert Frost expressed this idea about courage that can become a lifestyle when he penned the final lines of his famous poem "The Road Not Taken":

> Two roads diverged in a wood, and I—
> I took the one less traveled by,
> And that has made all the difference.

Once you start off on a courageous route, it often becomes easier to keep traveling than to turn back.

*Security is like the side of a swimming pool. We can use it to
cling to or to push off from.*   —TERRY SULLIVAN

COURAGE GROWS WHEN EXERCISED

A police officer shows up at your door. "I'm sorry to have to
bring you this news. Is someone here who can stay with you?
I hate to be the one to tell you like this. But it's your children—
they've just been killed by a sniper. A freak accident—while they
were eating at McDonald's."

Your doctor phones your office and asks someone to call you
out of a meeting: "Your tests results are back. I'm afraid I have
some bad news. You have cancer—a very advanced stage."

Your boss of ten years calls you into a closed-door meeting
after hours. "I'm making a little alteration to the books—that's
what I prefer to call it." He smiles at you, as if sharing an inside
joke. "It could get us ten to twenty years behind bars if the right—
or should I say wrong?—people discover it. But nobody except
you and me need know anything about it. And you just forgot
about it, right?"

If you wait until you need courage before you give it a
thought, it's too late. In the same way, you don't just one day go
out and decide you'll run a 10K race. Instead, you exercise a few
weeks or months before the event to strengthen your muscles
and build up your endurance so that you'll have it when you
need it. The same is true for being able to turn a major "crisis"
into an opportunity: The more you practice courage in smaller
situations, the more likely you will have strengthened your
"courage" muscles for the bigger situations and challenges.

Our fears rarely decrease with age. If anything, they multiply.
To a great extent, innocence and ignorance protect children—

what they don't know, they can't fear. Children fear the dark,
losing a doll, having to go to bed early, making a bad grade.
But adults cannot close their eyes to the potential for danger all
around them. Adults fear financial setbacks, debilitating disease,
loss of relationships, war, death.

The older you get, the more—not less—courage you need.
If you intend to have courage to face the tough stuff at seventy,
you'll need to start exercising long before you hit that milestone.

> *Old age isn't for cowards.*   —BETTE DAVIS

In addition to exercising your courage muscles to strengthen
them, you can increase your courage in other ways:

Focus on Your Power Supply

Instead of thinking about the obstacles, focus on the goal.
Instead of thinking about what you lack, focus on what God can
provide. During the September 11 terrorist takeover of United
Flight 93, Todd Beamer recited Psalm 23 with a telephone opera-
tor just before he and the other courageous passengers bolted
into action to save lives on the ground. He well understood the
source of his strength:

> *If God is for us, who can be against us?* (Romans 8:31)
> *Take heart! I have overcome the world.* (John 16:33)
> *I have set the Lord always before me. Because he is at my right hand,*
>   *I will not be shaken.* (Psalm 16:8)
> *Those who hope in the Lord will renew their strength. They will soar*
>   *on wings like eagles; they will run and not grow weary, they will*
>   *walk and not be faint.* (Isaiah 40:31)

Even when walking through the dark valley of death I will not be
afraid, for you are close beside me, guarding, guiding, all the way.
  (Psalm 23:4, TLB)
You will keep him in perfect peace, whose mind is stayed on You,
because he trusts in You. (Isaiah 26:3, NKJV)
Be strong and courageous. Do not be terrified; do not be discouraged, for
the Lord your God will be with you wherever you go. (Joshua 1:9)
He gives strength to the weary and increases the power of the weak.
  (Isaiah 40:29)
The Lord is with me; I will not be afraid. What can man do to me?
  (Psalm 118:6)
Everything is possible for him who believes. (Mark 9:23)
Let us then approach the throne of grace with confidence, so that we
may receive mercy and find grace to help us in our time of need.
  (Hebrews 4:16)
With God all things are possible. (Matthew 19:26)
I can do everything through [Christ] who gives me strength.
  (Philippians 4:13)

Remember Past Victories
Whenever you face a challenge, thinking about past successes
gives you confidence for the future.

We are more than conquerors through him who loved us.
  (Romans 8:37)
Remember that you were slaves in Egypt and that the Lord your God
brought you out of there with a mighty hand and an outstretched
arm. (Deuteronomy 5:15)
Remember the wonders he has done, his miracles, and the judgments
he pronounced. (1 Chronicles 16:12)

Act on Your Faith with Confidence

Receiving courage is not like taking an intravenous medication. You can't stretch out on a hospital bed, have the nurse insert the needle, wait until you feel the effects of the morphine, and then stand up and walk out of the hospital with confidence that the medication has conquered the pain and you can move about freely.

When it comes to courage, things happen in reverse order. You can't wait for guarantees. You first make up your mind to act. *Then* you feel courage flowing through your veins.

> *God did not give us a spirit of timidity, but a spirit of power, of love and of self-discipline.* (2 Timothy 1:7)
>
> *Do not let your hearts be troubled and do not be afraid.* (John 14:27)
>
> *Be strong in the Lord and in his mighty power. . . . Put on the full armor of God, so that when the day of evil comes, you may be able to stand your ground, and after you have done everything, to stand. Stand firm then.* (Ephesians 6:10, 13-14)

We express our faith in God verbally; then we act on that expression. When we put feet to our words, the courage will start to flow through our veins.

Shun Applause

After doing something courageous, be careful not to step into the spotlight and accept accolades for victories that God has granted. If you don't remember the source of your strength, courage can fade fast. Bravery builds from the mind-set of gratitude.

*I thank God for my handicaps, for through them, I have
found myself, my work, and my God.* —HELEN KELLER

Adding the Finishing Touches to Your Portrait

Students of art cannot continue to draw apples coming out of
fruit bowls or the ubiquitous meadow with a stream flowing
beside it. To progress in their art, they have to find the courage
to attempt more complex paintings.

Even seasoned artists must be bold to get their message
across in their work, and their patrons must be bold in sponsor-
ing them or displaying work that flies in the face of cultural
norms. Consider the courage of the first artist and patron who
hung a painting of black and white children together in the
same schoolroom. Consider the artist who painted a malnourished child in rags standing as a beggar among the wealthy.
Even unusual artistic techniques such as abstract sculptures
or the use of bold color combinations or strange angles require
courage.

In every discipline or walk of life, courage counts. So what
to do when you don't feel courageous? Act courageously anyway. Nobody but God can tell the difference. And he doesn't
care—as long as you act.

*The coward seeks release from pressure. The courageous
pray for strength.* —FRANCES J. ROBERTS

Without courage, wisdom bears no fruit.

—BALTASAR GRACIAN

A man without courage is a knife without an edge.

—BENJAMIN FRANKLIN

Adversity causes some men to break; others to break records.

—WILLIAM ARTHUR WARD

One man with courage makes a majority.

—ANDREW JACKSON

FIVE

COMPASSION
Looking at the Face in the Portrait

*W*hat is your first response toward weak and helpless people—compassion, avoidance, or pridefulness?

*H*ow do you most often express your compassion—with emotions or action?

"I FEEL so sorry for them."

"My heart goes out to anyone in that position."

"That news is like a death sentence. I can't imagine what I'd do in his situation."

"I just ache for those children."

"All his life he's struggled with a drinking problem. He just can't seem to hold a job, keep his family together, and get his life in order."

"She's devastated. I just wish I could say something that would help."

On first blush, compassion seems like a natural impulse when we hear of other people's struggles or pain. But after a

brief encounter or two with someone who is hurting, we sometimes tend to shy away because true compassion demands that
we watch others when they're stumbling, weak, vulnerable,
broken, hurt. Our spontaneous response to pain is either to fix
it or flee from it.

Jesus demonstrated compassion by healing people physically,
by telling them how to have a meaningful life and faith, and
ultimately by dying for them to heal their spiritual condition.
He showed compassion both by his emotions, as he listened to
people's needs and wept with his friends, and by his actions.
He demands the same from his followers and gives us a couple
of models in the parables of the Good Samaritan (see Luke 10)
and the Prodigal Son (see Luke 15). In fact, these parables are so
well known that the terms *Good Samaritan* and *Prodigal* have
slipped into our common vernacular.

Notice that these parables centered on the *acts* of compassion—not the *feelings* of compassion. The Good Samaritan is
memorialized because of his willingness to take the wounded
stranger to safety and pay for his medical treatment and lodging.
The Prodigal Son's father is memorialized not just because he
shed tears of joy at his wayward son's homecoming but because
he prepared an elaborate celebration. These men didn't just *feel*
compassion; they *acted* on their compassion.

Remember, people will judge you by your actions, not by
your intentions. As an old adage reminds us: "You may have a
heart of gold—but so does a hard-boiled egg." People's actions—
or inactions—are the best interpreters of their thoughts and
emotions. Our constructive work and creative imagination give
feet and fact to our feelings.

*Let us stop just saying we love people; let us really love
them, and show it by our actions.*   —1 JOHN 3:18, TLB

COMPASSION—A CAUSE OR A CURE?

Some would say that our society has "gone soft" on wrongdoers—
that compassion preached by misguided do-gooders is the reason
crime runs rampant in our society. Others counter that a lack of
compassion from small spheres of influence (family, friends) is
what forms criminals in the first place.

So where's the line between biblical compassion and forgiveness (offered "seventy times seven") and justice for the unrepen-
tant who represents a threat to others and to society as a whole?

Granted, individuals need to experience compassion throughout life. And in that sense, we can offer compassion to those in
distress or at risk. But compassion does not require careless
disregard for evil or justice or lack of punishment for those who
break the law or abuse others. Jesus had compassion on a sinful
world, but God's justice still required that Jesus pay the price for
sin with his death on the cross.

Our compassion may cause us grief and sadness. And it may
also cure that same grief. Our compassion may be just the thing
that touches someone in a difficult situation and gives them the
strength to struggle on. Our compassion can cure years of hurt
and motivate and compel someone to change a circumstance or
overcome a tragedy. But compassion does not necessarily overlook all wrongs done in society.

Where love is, God is.   —LEO TOLSTOY

Be imitators of God . . . and live a life of love.

—EPHESIANS 5:1-2

COMPASSION—CURTAILED BY ANGER, PREJUDICE, AND FEAR

At a time when the country was torn by racial strife and conflict over the issue of slavery, Abraham Lincoln put his presidency on the line—after he'd struggled for years to get elected. Much later, former president Lyndon B. Johnson concluded this about Lincoln's compelling political risk: "A singular quality about Abraham Lincoln . . . sets him apart from all our other presidents . . . a dimension of brooding compassion, love for humanity; a love which was, if anything, strengthened and deepened by the agony that drove lesser men to the protective shelter of callous indifference. . . . In what he did to lift the baleful burden of racism from the American soul, Abraham Lincoln stands as a teacher—not just to his people—black and white alike—but to all humanity."

Far too few people have such compelling compassion for individuals and groups unlike themselves: rich, poor, Hispanics, Asians, African Americans, Jews, Muslims, fundamentalists, liberals, male executives, female business owners, lawyers, priests, whatever group happens to be under suspicion. Anger toward one or more members from that group can destroy compassion. Fear of the power that a person or group holds over you or your future can stunt compassion. Finally, prejudice rooted for years in fear of the unknown or unfamiliar can stymie the expression of compassion.

In such instances, our imaginations may run away with us. Maybe we see a well-dressed, attractive redhead in the doctor's office, and we imagine that she has never had to work a day in her life, that she's living off a trust fund, that she flies to Acapulco every month to a health spa, that she has a full-time nanny for her children and an adoring husband who showers her with attention.

The reality may be that she was orphaned at age two, has worked since high school to put herself through college, has never had an extra penny to spend, makes her own clothes, and has just married the love of her life—a widower with two children who will give her grief for the next twenty years until they leave home.

Our imaginations and resulting resentments build entire profiles of individuals, committees, departments, organizations, nations, and races—all of which have no basis in reality. But these ruminations replace reality in our minds, and our compassion slips out the window.

COMPASSION—IS A TOUCH-UP CALLED FOR?

If you think you'd like to soften your outlook on the sea of humanity surrounding you, consider the following action plan.

Seek First to Understand the Sore Spot

When you see someone who's "trying your patience" (that is, someone toward whom you find it hard to extend compassion), before you start to judge their actions or inactions, first consider what has formed their own character. Make it a challenge to delve into their psyche to find the hurt that has festered into an oozing sore erupting into negative results ruining the lives of other people: What has been their upbringing? What hardships, disappointments, and pain have they had in life? Who have been their role models for direction in how to live?

Then consider their motivations and intentions in their current actions: Are their intentions to hurt others, or are their actions and decisions merely focused on a lifelong habit of self-protection?

Take Off Your Glasses or Get New Ones

"We don't see things as they are, we see things as *we are,*" observed French writer Anaïs Nin (1903–1977). Often we lack compassion for people because we see them as different. And that difference produces prejudice (prejudgment) because of fear. That fear, then, often leads to anger, which drives out any remaining fragment of compassion.

On those occasions all we need do is remove our glasses. We need to become aware of our prejudices and preconceived notions that color our view as passive onlookers into others' lives. Our own lenses strip us of an objective view and alter our perception of other people and their actions.

Take the Reins to Understand the Arena

"What she ought to do is . . ."

  "I tried to tell him that wouldn't work."

  "I don't see why she can't . . ."

  "There's no good reason that . . ."

  "Anybody should be able to . . ."

  "I don't think he really *wants* to improve the situation."

  "If you ask me, . . ."

Sound familiar? Most of us find it rather easy to tell other people how to run their lives and handle their tough situations.

And when they ignore the advice we've given them, our level of compassion drops even lower.

But I've discovered the quickest way to understand the depth of despair some people feel and to come to appreciate the difficulty they're in is to imagine myself calling the shots. For example, take my new friendship with Linda (not her real name).

Linda lives in Irving and attends an apartment Bible study near our church. She's awaiting trial for the homicide of her fifteen-year-old son, who was given an overdose of heroin by Linda's ex-boyfriend. Because the teen was a minor, the courts have held Linda responsible for the death. Unemployed and understandably depressed over the loss of her only child now that she has kicked the heroin addiction herself, Linda continues to ask for prayer and advice on what to do while she waits for her trial to come up.

Because I was eager to help her, my first thought was to pray with her and give her advice on things she could do to cope with the situation and turn her life around: learn a skill, get a job, stop living with her elderly parents, see a counselor—all my typical approaches to any problem: action. And when Linda didn't *do* any of those things, my first reaction was, *Why not? Doesn't she want to turn things around?*

But as I started to befriend her, I tried to imagine myself taking hold of the reins in her arena of life. Both her parents are elderly and ill. Now that I've met them, I understand that they *want* her living with them—they beg her not to move out but to stay and take care of them, every day, all day. How can she find time to learn a new skill and find a job? Who will hire her if she's honest about awaiting trial for murder—when she has to appear

in court every few weeks only to go through another postpone-
ment? And what is her obligation to her sister, whose husband
has just had a stroke and needs constant care and who frequently
asks her to stay with her and help out there for a couple of days
at a time?

I've come to understand that I might not find her situation
so "easy" to figure out myself. Everybody's life can't be cor-
rected by a couple of how-to books and a few sessions with
a counselor.

That's why Christ came and then sent the Comforter. Compassion from the rest of us can help soothe the jolts and pain
that so many people experience throughout life.

> *Love your enemies, bless those who curse you, do good to*
> *those who hate you, and pray for those who spitefully use*
> *you and persecute you.* —MATTHEW 5:44, NKJV

Adding the Finishing Touches to Your Portrait

Mary Cassat primarily painted female family members as they
went about their daily lives, having tea, reading a book in the
garden, or playing with their children. Leonardo da Vinci
revealed his love in his most famous painting, the *Mona Lisa*.
Other artists tell of falling in love with their subjects *as* they
painted them. Artists can even evoke feelings of compassion in
those who view their work by snapping a photograph of a starving child in a war-ravaged country, an abused wife on the streets
in Chicago, or a hardened criminal on death row.

All of us reveal our compassion—or lack thereof—as we play,

parent, perform on the job, profit in the marketplace, or prioritize our lives.

As you look at different people as potential recipients of
your compassion, study them with an artist's eye. Pay attention
to their faces, their hands, and particularly their eyes. Strive to
understand what they are really experiencing in the present and
what they may face in the future. What action could you take to
ease some of their pain, rewrite their story, and "retouch" their
countenance by showing compassion?

As you work in others' lives, your own character portrait will
reflect the same compassion you feel for your subjects.

> *Give, and it will be given to you. A good measure, pressed
> down, shaken together and running over, will be poured into
> your lap. For with the measure you use, it will be measured
> to you.*   —LUKE 6:38

> *We know that we have passed from death to life, because
> we love.*   —1 JOHN 3:14, NKJV

> *Love is life. . . . And if you miss love, you miss life.*
>   —LEO BUSCAGLIA

> *I am a little pencil in the hand of a writing God who is
> sending a love letter to the world.*   —MOTHER TERESA

SIX

LOYALTY

Displaying It under the Bright Light of Stress

*H*ow loyal are you under pressure?

*A*re you loyal to your enemies?

THE THOUGHT of a traitor in our midst triggers disgust. The confession of Robert Hanssen, a veteran FBI counterintelligence agent who sold highly classified national security information to the Russians and the former Soviet Union, shocked the nation in 2001. Betrayal is a nasty concept in most cultures, going all the way back to the ancient Greeks and Romans. Alternately, it has produced both anger and pain, as expressed by Julius Caesar's famous lament in Shakespeare's play *Julius Caesar,* when he was murdered: "*Et tu, Brute?*" (And you also, Brutus?), directed toward a man he had previously pardoned.

Aligning ourselves with the Robert Hanssens, John Walker Lindhs, Brutuses, or Judas Iscariots of the world would probably never enter our minds. We tend to think of loyalty in terms of its antithesis: *dis*loyalty or betrayal—some action that demonstrates our lack of loyalty, that visibly puts us on the other team.

Loyalty can refer to a static state—to remaining passively faithful to something: a person, an institution, an ideal, a cause, a custom, a product. But it means much more. The dictionary gives these synonyms: *conscientiousness, integrity, duty, devotion, honesty, obedience, submission, support, truthfulness, uprightness, ardor,* or *zeal.* Basically, we can narrow the characteristics into three categories. A loyal person shows faithfulness

1. through some effort,
2. with some enthusiasm, and/or
3. by behaving with what we'd call common decency in a given situation.

Loyalty isn't just the absence of an act of betrayal or *dis*loyalty; loyalty also refers to *acts* of *enthusiastic* support and protection. With that definition in mind, how loyal does your character portrait look? What are your acts of loyalty to your friends? to your parents? to your children? to your spouse? to your coworkers? to your employer? to your church? to God?

An ounce of loyalty is worth a pound of cleverness.

—ELBERT HUBBARD

LOYALTY TO THOSE YOU LOVE

Loyalty is essential to friendship. "The proper office of a friend is to side with you when you are in the wrong. Nearly anybody will side with you when you are right," Mark Twain once quipped.

Loyalty rates high among our reasons for choosing our friends. Friends always believe the best about you and refuse to let someone else's idle words ruin your reputation. They understand the contradictions that sometimes cause others to misunderstand you and your intentions, and they "run interference" when necessary.

Mark Twain's point granted, friends also show loyalty by protecting us even from ourselves occasionally. Sometimes true friends have the role of confronting us privately and holding us accountable when we get off track because they love us enough to endure our anger when they tell us the truth about ourselves or when they offer advice we don't want to hear. Friends sometimes become the voice of God in our lives.

Friends stay until the floodwaters of the crisis recede. They trust that the relationship will weather the storm of our temporary upset, any temporary moodiness, any lapse in our logic. They persevere in helping to meet our physical, emotional, and spiritual needs.

Friendships are nice when times are good; they become essential when times are difficult. Loyalty forms the primary color in our collection of friends.

> *Do not forsake your friend.*   —PROVERBS 27:10

> *A friend is always loyal, and a brother is born to help in time of need.*   —PROVERBS 17:17, NLT

LOYALTY TO THOSE YOU DON'T LIKE
You don't have to like someone to be loyal to that person.

In fact, that's often the principle behind the lump-in-the-throat part of some movies. The good guy and the bad guy have

been coworkers and friends for years. The bad guy does something outrageously horrible to the good guy and goes on the run
from the police. At the climax of the movie the good guy traps
the bad guy and has every opportunity to repay the wrong without anyone's ever finding out. Instead, the good guy lets him
walk away unharmed. If he hasn't up until this point, the hero
earns your respect. Having every reason to do wrong, the hero is
loyal to his former friend. The good guy may not like the bad guy
anymore, but he does him no harm.

We see that same kind of loyalty in David in the Bible. When
King Saul became jealous of his soon-to-be successor's growing
popularity, he began making life miserable for David, having his
men chase David around the countryside, trying to kill him when
he was out of the limelight. On two separate occasions David
came close enough to touch Saul, yet he spared Saul's life out of
loyalty and respect for him as God's anointed king (see 1 Samuel,
chapters 24 and 26). David was loyal to his king even when he
had every reason to turn his back on Saul.

Often the biggest deterrent to showing loyalty—whether to
friend or foe—is envy. People who, down deep, envy others' good
jobs, family lives, financial situations, appearance, intelligence,
social standing, or recognition—find it difficult to be loyal to
them. They may not do things actively to hurt them, but neither
do they go out of their way to protect them. In other words, they
may not start rumors about someone, but neither will they stop
them. They may not stand in the way of the promotion, but
neither will they initiate any steps to see that the other person
gets it. They will not bad-mouth the other person's accomplishments, but neither will they recognize the individual with a
letter or trophy at the industry meeting.

Envy, fear, and personal insecurity keep many people from developing this character trait of loyalty.

LOYALTY TO THOSE YOU SERVE

High schools and universities still earn the lifetime loyalty of their students. Many executors of wills discover that the deceased have left their estates to their alma maters. Other organizations, however, don't fare so well. Not only do they not inherit their former colleagues' or employees' money, neither do they win their personal goodwill.

In the last few years there has been an ever-widening circle of cynicism about large organizations and bosses "who don't have a clue," as evidenced by the enormously popular Dilbert cartoons created by Scott Adams. The massive layoffs and corporate scandals in the executive ranks during the last few years have also contributed to yet another rift growing in our culture. During the past decade it has become fashionable for employees to grumble about those in authority—their policies, their plans, their procedures, their expectations, their salary, the workload—and all the while, cashing their paychecks.

Granted, it is anyone's right—and sometimes even their ethical duty—to disagree about immoral or unethical acts. The difficult part of such a duty comes in accepting the sometimes hard situations and consequences. Otherwise, fulfilling that duty would not be difficult at all but only praiseworthy.

Loyalty means standing and supporting those you serve when they need your help. How refreshing to see students supporting their alma mater rather than defacing it. How refreshing to see employees vote to accept a salary decrease or

work long hours to keep the organization afloat through a difficult period. How refreshing to see loyal members of an organization defending and explaining a hard but morally right decision
to the public rather than remaining silent or jumping into the
fray of popular sentiment and cricitism.

Whoever eats my bread sings my song.   —HARRY COHN

Friends, employees, or members of our group or family show
loyalty simply by collecting information and passing it on to us.
They are like so many search engines on the World Wide Web.
We benefit from their interactions with others. Their network
becomes our network. Their perspective becomes our perspective.
If we don't have these loyal sources of information, we see and
know much less than we otherwise might. They help us multiply
our reach, our time, and our influence. Consequently, they protect us while they help us grow.

Part of loyalty is being an active conduit of information that
protects, warns, and informs for another's best interest.

There can be no friendship without confidence, and no
confidence without integrity.   —SAMUEL JOHNSON

LOYALTY UNDER PRESSURE

Loyalty goes unnoticed during lulls. It always surfaces more
clearly under stress. Here are some examples.

You and another person may have been friends for ten years
before an occasion arises that puts your loyalty to the test. For
the first time, your friend does something that causes your larger
circle of friends or work group to mistrust your friend's inten-

tions, and they don't believe her or like her anymore. How you react to the new pressure will be a test of your loyalty.

You have been an employee on your work team for several years. Two new people join the group and immediately begin to grumble about "how bad you have it" at the new place of business. You are all working on one key project and see each other daily to discuss issues relating to the work. They seem to be making sport of "the stupidity" of the executive decision maker of your key client, who will, in effect, be paying the salary of your team for the next eighteen months. How you react to the new pressure will be a test of your loyalty.

As long as your marriage is going well, there's no test of loyalty. But what about when you and your spouse find yourselves embroiled in conflict on all fronts—finances, careers, the kids, the in-laws, sex—and you don't even seem to like each other anymore? How you react to the pressure will be a test of loyalty to your marriage vows.

As long as your church friends live lives similar to yours, there's no test of loyalty. But what about when you think they're going astray, when they've lost their way, when they're beginning to engage in wrong activities? Do you speak up for what you believe? Do you remind them of what the Bible teaches about this or that issue—either by your words or your example? Or do you modify your own lifestyle and keep a lower profile? How you react to the pressure will be a test of loyalty to God.

Pressure is like so many drops of water. It drips. It puddles. It splashes. It floods.

Like betrayal, loyalty may show up at any time. But we see and appreciate it most clearly when it surfaces for an important cause, during a difficult situation, or to protect a faltering relationship.

Even in the face of grave danger, Queen Esther remained loyal to her people and saved her nation from annihilation. (See her story in the Old Testament in the book given her name.) Millions of descendants of Jews today still celebrate her success in saving them by her courageous deeds of loyalty.

Far more typically, we find just the opposite: people who believe in issues, causes, commitments—until the situation becomes difficult and demands personal action. For example, we see people who believe in the worthiness of a project or program—until someone asks for volunteers to lead the effort or write a check. People demand a certain benefit—until they're asked to vote on a tax bill to fund it. People believe in a cause—until it's time to put their jobs on the line or go to war to ensure that freedom or cause. But it's exactly such follow-through action that gives evidence of loyalty in the difficult situation.

> *Animals are reliable, many full of love, true in their*
> *affections, predictable in their actions, grateful and loyal.*
> *Difficult standards for people to live up to.*
> —ALFRED A. MONTAPERT

Adding the Finishing Touches to Your Portrait

The impressionistic painters such as Monet, Degas, Renoir, and others made a radical departure from popularly accepted techniques of their day. Their light-filled atmosphere, the brilliance of brushstroke, an unfinished quality about their work, and their choice of subject matter, which included landscape, portraiture, and still life, gave their work a distinctive flair.

But despite their own enthusiasm for experimentation in the new artistic techniques, the artists and their works were not immediately accepted by the general public. In fact, they could not even persuade museums and galleries to hang their paintings in the early days. This lack of support, however, led the "outcasts" to band together and exhibit their work on their own. They remained fiercely loyal to each other in the face of popular opposition, encouraging each other in their work and even offering financial support on occasion. In 1874, the first of these shows shocked the French artistic world, but by their last "renegade" exhibit in 1886, the artists had finally won their battle and major attention. Gauguin, Cézanne, Monet, Boudin, van Gogh, Degas, Renoir, Pissarro, and Sisley finally received recognition for their significant contribution to the artistic world.

Like these impressionistic painters, from time to time we, too, may be pressed to change our basic sense of what seems to work in any given situation in life. But our loyalty to an idea, a cause, or a person rarely shows up until it's challenged.

When analyzing your character portrait for loyalty, study it carefully for a sense of activity and movement. Notice, too, the richness of hue. When displayed under the bright lights of stress, does the color fade or shine more brilliantly?

Never does a man portray his own character more vividly, than in his manner of portraying another. —HENRI RICHTER

The best things in life are never rationed. Friendship, loyalty, love do not require coupons. —GEORGE T. HEWITT

SEVEN

PERSEVERANCE
"Touching Up" till the End

*A*re you typically the first person or the last to become discouraged and give up?

*D*o others call you an optimist or a pessimist?

*W*ill you ever deny your faith in God?

WE CAN HEAR *Keep the faith* or various translations thereof, on virtually any street around the globe. Religious faith serves as the bedrock of power, discipline, direction, and significance for every major religious group in the world. It is a strong force that binds all humanity together.

In 1902 William James, American psychologist and philosopher, published a major work titled *The Varieties of Religious Experience* to report the findings of his study of religious faith historically among all world religions. In his work he collected some two hundred personal narratives from those who had the most profound religious experiences and discovered they shared an almost universal "optimism." His work remains a classic in the field, and one critic has referred to it as a "thick stew of facts of experience" rather than philosophical speculation.

In other words, James dug to the heart of faith to see how it played out in the everyday lives of people—how did their walk, talk, and attitude track with what they said they believed? Their faith proved to be core to their existence.

Perseverance, or "faithfulness," appears in the apostle Paul's list of the fruit of the Spirit: "love, joy, peace, patience, kindness, goodness, faithfulness, gentleness, and self-control" (Galatians 5:22-23). And this same list of attributes has its parallels in all the major religions. As William Bennett points out in his best-seller *The Book of Virtues*, if there's one list of universally accepted admirable traits or goals among all faiths, this might be it. Since faithfulness refers to enduring or persevering to the end, it seems appropriate to end this part of the book on that trait from the list.

> *Faith is like a toothbrush. Every man should have one and use it regularly, but he shouldn't try to use someone else's.*
> —UNKNOWN

> *Being at peace with yourself is a direct result of finding peace with God.*
> —OLIN MILLER

PERSEVERANCE IN THE BIG THINGS

Perseverance, or faithfulness, applies both to the significant and the routine, to the difficult and the easy, to the visible and the invisible.

Perseverance means trusting God to provide for your needs

when you're without a job. Perseverance means crawling out of bed day after day, lifting a load of grief after you've lost a loved one. Perseverance means enduring physical pain when illness or accident strikes. Perseverance means waiting on God to judge your enemies when you've been falsely accused. Perseverance means making the right moral choices day after day, year after year, when no one might know if you make the wrong ones.

Perseverance means focusing on the significant when the trivial keeps tripping you. Perseverance means gearing your efforts toward the eternal when the temporary pays high dividends. Perseverance means showing gratitude instead of joining others in grumbling. Perseverance means trusting in God's control of the future even though others may despair.

> *Blessed is the man who perseveres under trial, because when he has stood the test, he will receive the crown of life that God has promised to those who love him.* —JAMES 1:12

PERSEVERANCE IN THE LITTLE THINGS
Sometimes people ask why God hasn't entrusted them with bigger opportunities and responsibilities. The answer may lie in their lack of faithfulness in the small things.

> *Faithfulness in little things is a big thing.*
> —JOHN CHRYSOSTOM

Perseverance means doing what you say you will do when you say you will. Perseverance means fulfilling the promise you made to your coworker about completing the project on time. Perseverance means showing up to coach a group of five teenagers, week after week after week. Perseverance means baking the casserole every third Tuesday to deliver to the assisted-living center because you said you would. Perseverance means spending every Thursday afternoon tutoring the child for whom English is a second language because he's depending on you to help him through second grade. Perseverance means having an upbeat attitude rather than a scowl. Perseverance means opening your home when someone needs a cold drink, a warm bed, and a listening ear. Perseverance means being consistent in meeting God alone in Bible study and prayer. Perseverance means doing whatever God has asked you to do day after day, decade after decade, year after year.

PERSEVERANCE PAYS

Defeat is but for a frequent, fleeting moment. Giving up is the only thing that makes it a permanent condition. No one wants to be labeled a quitter. We all extol the virtues of fortitude and stamina in exercising, dieting, and studying. But when it comes to spiritual pursuits, we don't as readily keep score. How many times have we started the "New Year's Resolutions" list with items such as maintaining a more consistent prayer time, spending more time with a special person, or working in the local mission at least once a month at the top of the list. Yet when we fail in our goals, we sigh, shrug it off, pat ourselves on the back for at least having good intentions, and pencil in the activity again on next year's list.

But perseverance pays off in spiritual matters as much as it does in any other area of consistency—or more so. In fact, the Bible commands it: "Let us not become weary in doing good, for at the proper time we will reap a harvest if we do not give up" (Galatians 6:9). In other words, God promises us a rich harvest if we persevere and "keep on keeping on."

> *Stopping at third base adds no more to the score than striking out.* —UNKNOWN

> *Do you approach things with the thought: "How can I make this work?" rather than "What happens if I fail?"*
> —BARBARA POPE

THE STAMINA TO KEEP ON KEEPING ON

Religious faith involves a deep relationship with God rather than a superficial one. Faith is more than agreeing with the truth, giving mental assent that God is the creator of the universe and controls life on earth. Faith in those facts represents a one-night stand.

But faithfulness is a commitment to obey and serve. If you are "faithful" to an organization such as your local parent-teacher organization, Mothers Against Drunk Driving, or your local Chamber of Commerce, you're committed to its mission, and you have pledged to serve it in some way. The same is true in your faithfulness to God.

To be faithful to the end is to serve to the end. Hebrews 11, often called the faith chapter in the Bible, doesn't describe faith with adjectives; it illustrates faith with the actions of faithful people. To paraphrase: By faith Abraham moved to a foreign land. By faith Noah built the ark. By faith the Israelites passed through the Red Sea on dry land. By faith Gideon fought the battle of Jericho. By faith Rahab risked her life to hide the spies.

God never gave us the option of sitting on the sidelines when it comes to faith. Jesus said, "He who is not with me is against me, and he who does not gather with me scatters" (Matthew 12:30). Faithfulness does not allow for staying on neutral ground. It involves commitment and service. Our strength comes from a day-to-day personal relationship with God. Not to decide is to decide.

Seek not to understand that you may believe, but believe that you may understand. —SAINT AUGUSTINE

GRATITUDE THAT GOD HAS THE SOURCE CODE

Notice that it was no short-term commitment for the heroes of the faith listed in Hebrews 11—Abraham, Isaac, Jacob, Joseph, Moses, and others. Verse 13 sums it up this way: "All these people were still living by faith when they died." Many didn't see the promises God had made to them fulfilled in their life-time. Still they didn't blink. Even though they couldn't see where God was leading, they followed his voice. Television cameras would never have captured them in the street demonstrating for more freedom—that is, freedom from God's complete authority in their lives.

I don't know about you, but I'd rather hold God's hand on the crowded highway of humanity than float along alone in complete freedom and risk stumbling to the ground and getting trampled by the traffic. Genuine faith is reassuring and enduring.

Our faith should be our steering wheel, not our spare tire.

—C. L. WHEELER

Our faithfulness, our perseverance, rests on our trust in God's ultimate sovereignty. When planes fly into buildings, . . . when dangerous bacteria are released into the population, . . . when snipers attack innocent victims in the streets, . . . when there is war in our land, . . . when disease strikes our loved ones, . . . when natural disasters destroy our businesses or our homes, . . . when evil people seem to get away with immoral practices, . . . when we are bone weary from feeding the hungry, . . . when we feel alone in our struggle to comfort our neighbor or our children, . . . that's when we must know deep in our souls that God wrote the source code for the universe.

He knows the schedule, the scheme, and the security codes for all users. When he decides to hit the END key, it's over. Time's up—either for all of us or individually. World's over. We win.

Always be prepared to give an answer to everyone that asks you to give the reason for the hope that you have.

—1 PETER 3:15

The just shall live by faith.   —HEBREWS 10:38, KJV

Adding the Finishing Touches to Your Portrait

Pablo Picasso lived to the age of ninety-one and produced more work in the last two decades of his life than at any other time. Some of the works from that period are dated not only by month and day but also by numerals indicating that the artist created multiple works on the same day. Picasso produced some of his finest paintings in his final days.

Georgia O'Keefe lived to ninety-eight. She continued working in pencil and watercolor until the age of ninety-four and produced objects in clay until she was ninety-six.

Michelangelo lived to the age of eighty-nine. He painted the fresco of the *Last Judgment* for the Sistine chapel between the ages of sixty-one and sixty-six—some thirty years after he did his monumental ceiling in the same chapel.

Claude Monet lived to the age of eighty-six. Even though he had trouble with failing eyesight in his later years, he had a special studio built on the grounds of his home so that he could work on huge canvases. He continued to give attention to his most famous theme—water lilies—and painted until the end of his life.

Masters all, they persevered in their work—to create, to grow—until their deaths. Serious artists continue to take in their surroundings with an artist's eyes—training themselves to notice detail, angles, color, or texture.

So it is in all of life: The faithful strive to persevere, endure, thrive, and finish strong. Living with faith is believing in the realities that have not yet happened. Trust God to guide your brushstrokes even when you can't see the canvas before you.

I do not pray for success, I ask for faithfulness.

—MOTHER TERESA

Let us run with perseverance the race marked out for us.

—HEBREWS 12:1

We know that all things work together for good to those who love God, to those who are the called according to His purpose.   —ROMANS 8:28, NKJV

Faith is not belief without proof, but trust without reservations.   —ELTON TRUEBLOOD

PART TWO

YOUR SIGNATURE
RELATIONSHIPS . . .
like writing a blockbuster

You enter the world with a certain cast of characters and with the plot already under way. But shortly after your starring role in the opening scene you begin to create your own scenes, select your own cast of characters for the starring and supporting roles, draft your own dialogue, and develop your own plot twists and drama. Granted, God directs the movie and serves as the final editor of your novel or screenplay, but you have great freedom as you write your life story.

Consider the scenes, settings, moods, and dialogues you have with family, friends, enemies, neighbors, and coworkers as your life unfolds. Your relationships often shape the plot and the outcome. Other characters will take their cues from you. If you work well together through the scene and script changes, Your Signature Relationships will become a vital source of support and strength.

Talent and dedication may take you to the top in most pursuits, but relationships and character keep you there.

To handle yourself, use your head; to handle others, use your heart.
                                                    —DONALD LAIRD

The easiest kind of relationship for me is with ten thousand people. The hardest is with one.
                                                    —JOAN BAEZ

A loving person lives in a loving world. A hostile person lives in a hostile world. Everyone you meet is your mirror.

—KEN KEYES JR.

When one is a stranger to oneself, then one is estranged from others too.   —ANNE MORROW LINDBERGH

EIGHT

SETTING THE SCENE
Being Kind to Your Kin and Colleagues

*A*re you known for being kind?

*C*an you change someone's actions toward you by showing kindness?

*C*an you change the way others see themselves, or can you make someone's life easier by practicing kindness?

"YOU HAVE a lot of trees back here," I said to Vernon one Sunday afternoon in his backyard after we'd been dating only a few months.

"Yes, I do."

"I thought you were going to be moving shortly."

"I probably will."

"So how long does it take them to grow? Won't you be moved before they're big enough to give you any shade?"

"Probably. But somebody will enjoy them after I'm gone." He moved the water hose over to a new base of roots. "I always plant trees wherever I live."

"Hmmm." It seemed like a waste of time to me. I enjoy gardening about as much as I love scrubbing a dirty skillet.

"Did I tell you about the man who helped me set out all these trees?"

I shook my head, and he related the following story.

SHOWING KINDNESS TO STRANGERS

Vernon sat watching the old man across the narrow aisle as he relished his fried chicken and dabbed his napkin at the corners of his mouth as an afterthought for the sake of onlookers. The mom-and-pop restaurant, in its out-of-the-way location, drew only locals, even for Sunday lunch. Vernon often stopped there to grab a bite on his way home from church. It was the kind of place where the owners called you by name and remembered that you liked gravy on the side.

With his battered suitcase beside him, it was obvious the elderly diner had walked over from the bus station across the street. Always intrigued by people who have a story, Vernon noticed that the old man had finished his lunch but didn't seem to be in any hurry to leave. The man lingered over his glass of water, watching other diners as they came and went, occasionally moving his suitcase from side to side to prevent someone tripping as they passed among the tightly arranged tables. He seemed amused by the children flying airplanes over the plates while their parents coaxed them to eat. The twinkle in his eye seemed to reveal memories of family days gone by.

Vernon took his last swig of iced tea and asked the older man, "Are you visiting someone here in Kingwood?"

"No. Just passing through."

"Where are you from?"

"Philadelphia." He paused for a moment, as if to assess Vernon's real interest in his itinerary. Deciding it was genuine, he elaborated. "My wife died a few weeks ago. Been married fifty-two years. Decided I needed a change. Got all my belongings here in this case." He patted the bent brown bag as if it were a collie dog. "Yeah, going out to live with my son."

That much information in such a brief exchange was just the kind of thing my husband, Vernon, needed to build a two-hour conversation. Although women are often said to have a special antenna for collecting information, Vernon does an admirable job himself. The old man's response was one of those thumbnail sketches that wallop you on the side of the head with the same kind of impact you sometimes get from a movie. A tidbit of classroom discussion from college English popped into my mind as I visualized the old man seated in the restaurant that day, with his life in his luggage.

Ernest Hemingway often discussed the importance of brevity in short-story writing when he had someone challenge him on the issue. He wagered that he could write a story in six words. His colleague took him up on the bet.

Hemingway wrote: "For sale: Baby shoes. Never used."

As Vernon later related the incident at the restaurant to me, I could still hear the leftover mark of sadness in his voice when he explained, "So I asked the old man to come home with me for the afternoon."

"You what? A total stranger?"

"He had nowhere else to go," Vernon said as he continued telling the story:

"Where's your son live?" he asked the old man.

"He's out in San Diego—or somewhere near there. That's where he's meeting my bus."

"Nice place," Vernon said as he finished his tea and started to get up to pay his check. "So are you going to have time to walk around here and see a little of the city before you go? They've got some great walking trails near here."

The old man shook his head.

"What time does your bus leave?"

"Ten o'clock tonight."

"You have to wait nine hours?"

"Bus is not the best way to travel, I guess. But it's cheap." The old man smiled, not at all bitterly.

"Why don't you come home with me for the afternoon, and I'll bring you back to catch your bus at ten? That's too long for you to have to sit here and wait."

The old man seemed to search Vernon's face for sincerity. "I wouldn't want to impose. I could just sit here probably another couple hours and then mosey on back over to the bus station."

"No, that won't be comfortable. I don't live far away. Got a little garden at home. I wasn't planning on doing anything special—just planting a few trees. I could use some help."

The old man's face lit up. "Oh, now that—yeah, I could help you do that. I know about planting trees." And with that, he reached for his luggage and followed Vernon out of the restaurant.

One kind act will teach more love of God than a thousand sermons.
—UNKNOWN

Once in the backyard, after Vernon had given him some of his own old work clothes to change into, the old man seemed much younger. "If you want some advice, I'd tell you to stagger those trees," he said as Vernon was about to dig the second hole.

"What do you mean?"

"Like this." The visitor took the extra shovel and began to mark the spots across the back lawn. When he returned to where Vernon was standing, he gave him the reason: "The roots don't crowd each other that way, and they get more sunlight."

"I see," Vernon said appreciatively. "Nobody ever told me that before. Makes sense. Let's do it, then."

They set out nine trees before dark. In between, they shared their lives.

When they'd finished, Vernon showed him to the extra shower so he could clean up and change back into his traveling clothes. He took him out for dinner on the way back to the bus station for his ten o'clock departure. As they parted, they exchanged phone numbers and vowed to keep in touch.

But Vernon never heard from the man again.

Four years later, Vernon received a letter from the old man's son, telling him that his father had recently passed away. The letter said, in part: "My father never stopped talking about you and your kindness to him that Sunday afternoon. He was truly amazed that in this day and time someone would invite him as a stranger into their home—and make him feel useful. That was the best part. I found your address in his room and thought I should let you know what your kindness had meant to him. He talked of you and that day often, as if you were old friends."

As Vernon told me the story while watering the trees spread

across his lawn, I understood that they had indeed been friends—
even if for only a day.

Kindness is called for even when there is no commonality
other than the human connection.

> *"I was hungry and you gave Me food; I was thirsty and you*
> *gave Me drink; I was a stranger and you took Me in; I was*
> *naked and you clothed Me; I was sick and you visited Me;*
> *I was in prison and you came to Me." Then the righteous*
> *will answer Him, saying, "Lord, when did we see You hungry*
> *and feed You, or thirsty and give You drink? When did we see*
> *You a stranger and take You in, or naked and clothe You?*
> *Or when did we see You sick, or in prison, and come to You?"*
> *And the King will answer and say to them, "Assuredly, I say*
> *to you, inasmuch as you did it to one of the least of these My*
> *brethren, you did it to Me."*   —MATTHEW 25:35-40, NKJV

THE POWER OF PLANNED KINDNESS
PROVES POSITIVE

Conari Press published a book in 1993 called *Random Acts of
Kindness,* which was a collection of true stories of people observ-
ing and experiencing kindnesses shown toward others, many
of whom were total strangers. The book quickly became a
national best-seller, and the title and theme became part of
our vernacular. People long to believe that such attitudes and
behaviors still exist in our culture today.

But in addition to such random acts, consider planned kindness. If random acts can produce such enormous good in people's
lives, imagine what planned acts in the lives of those we know and
love can do to change a relationship or a perspective.

*Kind looks, kind words, kind acts, and warm handshakes—
these are secondary means of grace when men are in
trouble and are fighting their unseen battles.*   —JOHN HALL

Coach Gary Robinson teaches a course called Teen Leadership for ninth graders at Coppell High School. He makes quite an impression on surly students when they enter his room for the first time: he stands by the door and greets each one by name with a handshake. He has continued the gesture each day of the school year.

On the days when he's otherwise occupied between class periods, he has a student take his place at the classroom door, shaking hands and greeting fellow classmates as they arrive. Why? He's teaching leadership. If the students want to influence people, they must recognize and show respect for others individually. Considering the uniqueness of this greeting from their teacher and the impression it has created, his students insist that this small act of courtesy has yielded big dividends.

The power of planned kindness proves positive for both givers and receivers. The receivers come to realize that they're important to you and worthy of respect. The givers respect themselves for the time invested and the discipline it takes to show kindness—possibly even in the face of insult or disregard.

Both givers and receivers share in the candlelight glow of courtesy.

*Nothing is ever lost by courtesy. It is the cheapest of the
pleasures, costs nothing and conveys much. It pleases him*

*who gives and him who receives, and thus, like mercy, it is
twice blessed.*   —ERASTUS WIMAN

KINDNESS CAN BE CONTAGIOUS

The line was long, and the Wal-Mart in Cleburne, Texas, was
hectic on Christmas Eve, according to the story by J. R. Labbe
in the *Fort Worth Star-Telegram*. Dozens of people stood at
the checkout lines with baskets of clothes, cameras, toys,
candy, electronics, and appliances, waiting to pay their tab
and wrap their treasures to slip under the tree for Christmas
morning.

Cashier Jeffrey Kandt looked up to scan the bar codes on
the next person's purchases. The woman standing there in well-
worn clothes pushed a PlayStation 2 toward him. It was her only
purchase. With calloused hands she began to pat herself down
for her money. A look of panic spread over her face, and her voice
rose as she searched.

It was the only gift her son had asked for. She had saved all
year for this. With tax, the total would come to $220, and she
had it—or, she did have it earlier that day. Where was the money?
She began to cry.

Cashier Kandt stood staring. A cashier's and manager's worst
nightmare on Christmas Eve. *Why me?* he thought. *Why my line?
Why tonight? I'm going to have to shut down the whole line and call the
manager until we get this sorted out.*

Then it happened. From the back of the checkout line, people
were passing money forward. A ten-dollar bill here. A five-dollar
bill there. A wad of ones. A check for $50 made out to Wal-Mart.
A collection of $220 finally reached the register, and an aston-
ished mother left with her son's Christmas-morning treasure.

Who primed the pump? Which five dollars started the action? What spark of impulse made that mother and child's Christmas—and year? Kindness multiplies when it motivates others to model the moment. One of us can make all of us better.

MANNERS MATTER: DON'T GO AWAY MAD—JUST GO AWAY!

We are at our best when we are being kind and generous to strangers—innocent strangers, kind strangers. But one of the most difficult places to be kind is at home around family members. The reasons may vary: We take them for granted and think they'll love us anyway. We think they're not worth the effort. We spend so much time with them that familiarity breeds irritability.

Whatever the cause, rudeness has destroyed many family relationships. The revival of respect and kindness could revolutionize others.

Rude? Who me? In case there's any question, here are some of the ways we show discourtesy or a lack of kindness at home:

- not speaking to others when you enter a room
- failing to return a greeting when someone speaks to you
- not telling a family member where you're going or how you can be reached in an emergency
- not telling someone when you expect to return
- borrowing others' things without asking
- not returning items in good condition after borrowing them
- sulking and not talking when you're in a bad mood
- using a harsh tone when speaking

- slamming a door in someone's face
- not writing down phone messages, assuming you'll remember—and then forgetting to pass them on
- dressing inappropriately when others have friends over
- leaving food and beverages sitting around in common areas
- not offering to help others carry a heavy load
- not offering to lower the volume if the sound is disturbing others
- switching TV channels without asking when someone else is watching
- using sarcasm or put-down humor meant to embarrass others on sensitive issues
- failing to say please and thank you or express other pleasantries such as asking how others are feeling when they've been sick or asking how their day has gone

Love is patient, love is kind. . . . [Love] is not rude.
—1 CORINTHIANS 13: 4-5

These represent just the basic discourteous behaviors that colleagues or friends would never expect from us in the workplace or at school. But on the job and in the community in general, these additional small acts of rudeness creep in to annoy others, to demean and show disrespect to them, and they finally weaken or break the relationship and lessen our influence with them:

- showing up late to a meeting and disrespecting others' time
- speaking to some people but not others in a group
- "dressing someone down" in front of others so as to embarrass and humiliate that person

- excluding others from a group when getting together for
  breaks or for lunch simply because you feel they are not
  equal to you socially or intellectually

> *Kind words are the music of the world. . . . It seems as if*
> *they could almost do what in reality God alone can do—*
> *soften the hard and angry hearts of men. No one was ever*
> *corrected by a sarcasm—crushed, perhaps, if the sarcasm*
> *was clever enough, but drawn nearer to God, never.*
>
> —FREDERICK WILLIAM FABER

The opposite of these actions, of course, are the small kindnesses
that convey respect for others, lift their spirits, build their self-
esteem, make their burdens lighter, and increase your influence
with them, ultimately when you have an important belief or
value to share.

Over time, kindness can pry open a hard or hurting heart.

> *Be kind and compassionate to one another.*
>
> —EPHESIANS 4:32

TESTING 1 . . . 2 . . . 3 . . .

Before scriptwriters air the final versions of their movie and put
it "in the can," they often hold private screenings to get audience
reactions. They're looking for feedback on characterizations,
pacing, plot, and so forth that they can alter with minor editing
before the final release. You might want to consider the following
tests in creating your signature relationships before you write
final scripts:

Test 1 (for family members): As a college student, would I treat others at my school this way? As an employee or employer, would I treat others in the workplace this way?

Test 2 (for work or family behavior): Would I want someone to write up this behavior in the school or corporate newsletter? Would I want this profile posted in video or Webcast on the Internet?

Test 3 (for family behavior): Would I be hesitant for my family members to talk candidly with my work friends and tell them what it's like living with me at home?

Test 4 (for family behavior): What would my family members say about me at a roast on my next birthday—if they were completely honest?

Test 5 (for family or work behavior): If I were a victim of a terrorist attack or a sudden car accident tomorrow, what would be their last memory of me?

Test 6 (for family or work behavior): If I watched a movie starring myself, would I really like the main character?

Adding the Finishing Touches to Your Blockbuster

All successful novels share one common ingredient: a likable hero or heroine with a good heart. Create a scene where the main character kicks a dog or abuses a child, and you have lost a reader and doomed a book to failure—no matter how intriguing the plot or romantic the setting. Main characters can have other flaws, exercise poor judgment, and wreak havoc with poor decisions, but they can't be mean or unkind. In fact, a novelist may create a serial killer who happens to love his cocker spaniel or help little old ladies across the street and then uses those kindnesses to create an undercurrent of empathy for him with the reader.

Your reactions to the test questions in the previous section may lead you to rewrite some of the scenes that routinely play out in your home or workplace. If you do rewrite the dialogue you use, typically those on the receiving end will take their cues from you.

In real life, too, we want to know that others around us "have a good heart" despite their wrong actions or decisions. Their good heart becomes evident in all the little things that unfold day by day. As you work on setting the scene for your signature relationships, strive to make sure the main character in your life story has a kind heart.

Life is not so short but that there is always time for courtesy.
—RALPH WALDO EMERSON

Kindness is the golden chain by which society is bound together. —GOETHE

People will overlook the faults of anyone who is kind.
—UNKNOWN

If you have some respect for people as they are, you can be more effective in helping them to become better than they are. —JOHN GARDNER

Kindness is love in work clothes. —UNKNOWN

NINE

DRAMATIC DIALOGUE
Telling and Hearing the Truth

*A*re your relationships with others strong enough so that they trust and accept your honest, direct communication on personally sensitive issues?

*C*an you listen without being defensive when others tell you about your own weaknesses and suggest ways you might want to change?

"I DON'T think Mom and Dad are well enough to make the trip across country to the family reunion. One of us should talk them out of trying to go before they buy airline tickets," Caroline mentioned to her sister when she telephoned during her lunch hour.

"That's your department," Tabby said. "I never wanted to have the family reunion in Oregon in the first place."

"Well, that decision was already made last year. I'm just focusing on doing what's best for them now since the surgery.

The doctor told Dad that he needed to stay with his physical therapy three times a week to get his strength back."

"You've been calling the shots all along," Tabby said. "No need to change now. Just tell them you want them to stay home."

"It's not about what I want. I'm concerned about what's best for them," Caroline insisted. "I brought it up to see if you agreed. If you do, then I thought we could talk to them together, maybe this weekend, or even go over there tonight. They've got their hearts set on making the trip, but I thought they'd more likely listen to both of us."

"You go ahead. I'm working late tonight."

"I'll wait until you can get off and have dinner," Caroline said.

"Look. What's the point? If you don't want them to go to the family reunion, just say so. You control the checkbook anyway."

"Look, I *want* them to go." Caroline tried once again to clarify. "I just don't think they're physically up to it."

"You want me to break the news so they can be angry with me rather than you—is that it?"

"Why would I want them to be angry with you?" Caroline asked.

"You've got your reasons, I'm sure. One of which probably has to do with Dave. I'm sure he's somehow involved in all this, because he always is. He never manages to show up for anything and still manages to ruin everything about our family."

"Forget it. I'll talk to Mom and Dad myself."

We go out of our way *not* to communicate with people with whom we feel out of step or disconnected. Just as in the conversation between sisters Caroline and Tabby, we manage to talk all around the issues—jabbing, poking, tempting, hiding, masking, withdrawing, sulking—but never communicate honestly and directly about the real issues.

These sisters haven't effectively "twist-tied" their communication. Imagine a character in a movie dashing into the kitchen to make a sandwich. Consider how he closes the bag of bread. When he's in a hurry, he grabs the plastic bag with one hand, grabs the tie in the other hand, gives the bag a twist or two, and tosses it aside. The bag, still bulging with air, will burst if anything sharp punctures it. If the character opens and closes the bag often enough without squeezing out the excess air, he'll soon have a stale loaf of bread.

By the same token, Caroline and Tabby have "twist-tied" their communication with all the stale air inside. That is, they've never let out the stale, pent-up emotion sufficiently to open the way for honest dialogue. Instead, on occasion, when it's necessary to talk about an event or issue—in this case, their parents' trip—they open the bag just long enough to twist together a few lines of dialogue while a few puffs of pent-up emotion escape. Then they tie it all up again or seal off the discussion until next time. They never clear the air out of the bag. They never talk through the issues—they just keep tying their emotions up inside, letting them get stale and ruin the loaf.

On the other hand, another character might be more careful in closing the bread bag. She might take her time to close up the loaf of bread the proper way, squeezing most of the excess air out of the plastic bag before she starts to tie it shut. Then as she twists the tie, she gradually deflates the bag, eliminating any chance for puncture. The bread fits snugly inside the bag.

You can learn to communicate the same way, listening to pent-up emotions before twisting hearts and minds together in a common bond or task. Trying to communicate any other way is an exercise in futility.

LISTEN BEFORE YOU UNLOAD

In order to move along the story line, characters in your movie eventually have to talk to each other to tackle the problem. Otherwise, it becomes a comedy of errors, misunderstanding after misunderstanding after misunderstanding. Although such miscommunication may keep us laughing at the movies, it can make us cry in real life.

Too many conversations focus on face saving rather than problem solving. In close relationships we have to establish an environment where our family and friends know they can be direct and honest with us. Not brutal, rude, or unkind. Just honest. And there is a difference. We'll talk more about that later.

Our socialization in other settings—school, work, church, community—may have led us to shy away from direct, honest communication. A friend in a new suit asks us, "How does this outfit look?" We say, "Fine," even if we think it doesn't fit well and the color makes the wearer look sick. We even laugh at jokes we don't think are funny just to lessen another's discomfort with silence. These niceties make general camaraderie possible.

But in the workplace or community, those social norms and rituals can undermine valid communication and the giving and receiving of honest feedback. Ray, a friend and vice president of a large consulting firm, was conducting a performance review. In his attempt to be diplomatic with an employee who was not performing up to standard, he "explained" why they were transferring her to a branch office. In response to his vague, circuitous explanation, she asked for a raise.

> *One of the surest marks of good character is a man's ability*
> *to accept personal criticism without malice to the one who*
> *gives it.*   —O. A. BATTISTA

In family matters these same social norms and expectations can stifle character growth. Defensiveness crops up to stop the truth. We face a dilemma: We can either communicate honestly—which may correct a problem but break a relationship—or protect a relationship, even if the communication sends a dishonest message, prevents character growth, and covers up a bigger problem.

Only when we learn to let comments lie on the table, without counterattack, defensiveness, or denial, do others learn that it's acceptable to communicate honestly and openly with us. And only then can effective discussion follow. Each of us must let important people in our lives know that it's acceptable and even desirable to tell the truth *as they see it* in love and harmony.

Once we've created that atmosphere and those parameters in our relationships with family, friends, coworkers, and neighbors, we can then engage in the real dialogue that produces dynamic change.

> *A word aptly spoken is like apples of gold in settings of silver.*
> —PROVERBS 25:11

> *A smile in giving honest criticism can make the difference*
> *between resentment and reform.*   —PHILIP STEINMETZ

Returning to the "bag of bread" idea, to create that open atmosphere you have to let the hot air escape before you try to close up the bag around the bread. As we learn to listen, we encourage others to talk.

Listen to understand, not to refute. Listen to things that are difficult to hear. Listen without correcting the speaker. Listen without denial. Listen without defense. Listen without counter-attack.

> *He who answers before listening—that is his folly and his*
> *shame.* —PROVERBS 18:13, NKJV

When other people unload their pent-up emotion, you'll begin to understand their motivations, intentions, perspective, facts, interpretation of the facts, and conclusions about the facts. Once they have listened to themselves explain their thoughts and feelings, they'll come to a better self-understanding, reduce their stress, and appreciate you more for the gift of listening and understanding.

After you've listened well and verified to them that you've heard exactly what they've said and what they're feeling about what they've said, they will feel obliged to hear what you have to say about the situation. In fact, after you know so much about the situation and come to such a deep understanding of their motives, intentions, goals, and feelings, they'll often ask for your analysis of the situation, your conclusions, and even your advice for what they should do.

Then you have your invitation to influence. It is far easier to persuade others with your ears than with your tongue. You've gathered the data—their feelings, their perspective, their input—from them, the official source. By listening to them, you have earned the right to communicate the truth *as you see it* in love.

> *Sometimes you have to be silent to be heard.*
>
> —STANISLAW J. LEC

DIRECT DOESN'T MEAN DOWN AND DIRTY

Never confuse direct, straightforward communication with bluntness. Bold communication involves breaking bad news or bringing up sensitive issues that might be difficult to handle well but that have high payoff value if the discussion proves productive. Bluntness, on the other hand, is careless communication. It involves bringing up potentially sensitive situations without regard for wording, tone, or timing. Notice the contrast in the following examples:

> *Bold:* "I wanted to discuss the issue of the money missing from the petty cash drawer."
> *Blunt:* "I wanted to talk to you about what you did with the money from the petty cash drawer."

> *Bold:* "I'm disappointed that you want to drop out of college."
> *Blunt:* "College dropouts are quitters."

> *Bold:* "You promised me you wouldn't accept another job that required us to move out of state."
> *Blunt:* "You lied to me about accepting another job out of state."

Bluntness shuts down dialogue. Boldness opens it. Bluntness reveals hostility. Boldness conveys hope. Bluntness lacks forethought. Boldness takes courage. Bluntness sabotages success. Boldness initiates response.

> *Remember not only to say the right thing in the right place, but far more difficult still, to leave unsaid the wrong thing at the tempting moment.* —BENJAMIN FRANKLIN

> *The tongue has the power of life and death.*—PROVERBS 18:21

SPEAKING IN TRUTH, NOT TIRADES

Some people mistakenly think that their opinion or view is the only "realistic" one. They often preface their comments with, "Let's get real here about X." Or, "You've got to face reality about Y." Or, "Let's be more realistic and deliberate about the situation." Or, "Let's plug in more realistic or appropriate numbers than what you're using if we're going to discuss this seriously."

In the way they've framed your comments with theirs, they communicate that you are creating "fantasy" and they are sharing "fact." The difference often comes through in attitude. Realism focuses on facts; gloom comes from attitude. If you must disagree, try to do so without being disagreeable.

> *It is much easier to be critical than correct.*
> —BENJAMIN DISRAELI

Fact, Fiction, and Faction

For years, novelists and journalists worked in two different worlds: Novelists dealt with fiction and often did not feel compelled to stick with the facts. Journalists, on the other hand, were bound by facts and prided themselves on objective reporting. All that changed when Truman Capote penned his bestseller *In Cold Blood* and called it "faction." He defined the genre as a mixture of fact and fiction, a true story fleshed out with imagination about the facts and real conversations that were impossible to know because the only people who really know what occurred are dead.

Conversations, in general, are sometimes like Capote's faction—a mixture of truth and fiction. That is, after they're over, everybody has a different viewpoint on exactly what was said.

When you're discussing serious, sensitive issues, generally everybody has a viewpoint. It's only natural to see your own viewpoints, conclusions, and interpretations as factual or valid and those of the other person as opinion and invalid. The real "truth" typically falls somewhere in the middle.

> *The truth does not change according to our ability to stomach it emotionally.*   —FLANNERY O'CONNOR

DO YOU NEED A SCRIPT REWRITE?

Nagging has never worked. Otherwise, those hearing it wouldn't have labeled it "nagging"; they would have called it "reminding." Perspective marks the difference between the two—speaker or listener. If you're to the point of nagging (in the other person's point of view), the listener has tuned out. It's time to rewrite the script because the other person is no longer picking up the cues. Determine why the other person is no longer listening, and then decide on another approach to get your point across.

In writing your dialogue scenes for your blockbuster, consider reframing the context of the conversations from negative to positive. Have you noticed that when relationships are strained, conversations tend to get off track easily and focus on everything but the real issues that need to be resolved? You spend all the energy and time on the meaningless bickering and never focus on the core problem.

The Bible provides several great models of "rewriting the script" in such conversations. Jesus approaches the Samaritan woman at the well (John 4) and asks her for a drink of water. During the course of their conversation, she tries to discuss everything but the central issues. She brings up the racial discord of the day between the Jews and the Samaritans: "You are a Jew and I am a Samaritan woman. How can you ask me for a drink?" Jesus sidesteps the racial issue with, "If you knew the gift of God and who it is that asks you for a drink, you would have asked him and he would have given you living water" (vv. 9-10).

On another occasion, the religious leaders of the day brought a woman accused of adultery to Jesus and shoved her to the ground in front of him: "Teacher, this woman was caught in the act of adultery. In the Law Moses commanded us to stone such women. Now what do you say?" (John 8:4-5). In replying, Jesus "rewrote the script." He redirected the conversation from her adultery to the condition of all humanity: "If any one of you is without sin, let him be the first to throw a stone at her" (John 8:7). When the woman's accusers got Jesus' drift, they slipped away. Then he commanded the woman to give up her lifestyle and forgave her for what she had done in the past.

Script rewritten. Point made. Scene changed. Accusers gone. Woman forgiven.

If the dialogues in your own relationships seem to be going

in circles, consider rewriting the script—recreate the difficult messages in a positive context rather than in a negative one. Instead of arguing with your daughter about the disadvantages of dropping out of school, rewrite the dialogue from a positive perspective—talk about the advantages of staying in school. Instead of talking about how irresponsible Mac has been to the team project, rewrite a more positive dialogue—talk about how to hold Mac more accountable on the team project. Instead of arguing that your spouse's jealousy is creating embarrassment and leading you to the brink of divorce, change the script to create a more positive conversation—discuss how you might be contributing to your spouse's feelings of insecurity or how you could help your spouse feel more secure in your marriage relationship.

People respond better to positive programming than to negative. If the characters in your own life story always seem intent on discussing issues from a negative perspective, rewrite your script.

How forceful are right words!   —JOB 6:25, NKJV

Adding the Finishing Touches to Your Blockbuster

Novels or movies are structured according to scenes; the plotline unfolds through a series of scenes. And by and large each scene centers around dialogue. Some dialogue "sets the stage" for action that will follow. Some dialogue characterizes. Some dialogue builds suspense.

For the most part, behavior change results from a dramatic event and related dialogue—one spouse tells the other, "I still love you no matter what," or the doctor tells the hero he has two months to live, or the grandmother tells the grandson it's time to accept responsibility and support his wife and baby. Someone gets hit between the eyes with truth at a point of decision; some comment to the main character serves as the turning point in his or her life. The same thing happens in real life. Honest, loving communication produces perspective and change.

Nothing proves more crucial to the way your life story unfolds than the relationships you build along the way. And the essence of all your relationships is your conversations running end to end, from the first to the final scene. Listen willingly. Interpret perceptively. Speak honestly. Phrase lovingly. Position positively. Edit carefully.

> *Words are, of course, the most powerful drug used by mankind.*
>
> —RUDYARD KIPLING

> *The tongue that brings healing is a tree of life.*
>
> —PROVERBS 15:4

> *Find someone who is willing to share the truth with you.*
>
> —JIM ROHN

> *He who guards his lips guards his life, but he who speaks rashly will come to ruin.*   —PROVERBS 13:3

TEN

CREATING THE MOOD
Building Connection and Chemistry

*W*ill the emotional bonds you've built among your family members hold you together during difficult times?

*H*ow successful are you in encouraging people to pull together as a team?

THE MOVIE opens with Kirk and Jason eating hot dogs at a ball game. In the next scene their car gets stuck in the mud on a country road and they have to walk ten miles to get help. As the plot moves along, such throwaway scenes continue: Jason takes a message from Kirk's mother-in-law and "lays it on thick" about how respected Kirk is at work. In the next scene, Kirk commiserates with Jason when his wife walks out on him. So at the movie's climax, when Kirk is dying and needs a kidney transplant and Jason offers to donate a kidney even though it means he'll be off work long enough to lose his job, we find the scene totally plausible. The previous "small" scenes have created the emotional connection between the two main characters that makes the climax believable.

Connections in real life happen the same way: In writing your own life story, you have to build emotional bonds before you need them. Take a look at the following "scenes."

"Hello?" Katrina answered on the first ring, hoping to intercept a call from the doctor's office before her fifteen-year-old daughter monopolized the phone until bedtime.

"Madison, it's for you." She held the receiver and waited for her daughter to appear from behind her bedroom door. "It's Carrie. Take it down here."

"Why?"

"Why not?"

"Because I don't want to."

"What's such a secret that you can't talk about it in front of me?"

Madison smirked.

Katrina still held the phone out toward her.

"Why do I have to take it down there?"

"Because I said to."

Madison grabbed the phone. "Carrie, I can't talk now." She hung up. "May I leave the room now?"

"No, I want to talk to you."

"About what?"

"Your grades."

"What about them?"

Katrina held Madison's progress report of all Ds toward her. "They were all Bs last time. Look at them."

"I already have."

"So why have they fallen so low this period?"

"I don't know. Ask the teachers."

"Can they tell me?"

"Probably not."

"Why not?"

"I don't know."

"Who does?"

Shrug.

Katrina raised her voice. "Tell me what's going on with you!"

"I'll tell you what's going on with me. You want to know what's going on with me? I'll tell you what's going on with me! I'm tired of hearing everybody—you and Daddy—scream and fight around here every night. You sound like a witch—"

"Don't you talk to me like that. Go to your room."

Madison marches back upstairs and slams the door.

A teenager closed down, a mother-daughter relationship waiting to break.

Shannon reached up to flip the Out sign beside her name on the white board as she hurried through the reception area. Missed. She tried again on tiptoes. A third time. Finally she resorted to going around behind the counter and making the switch.

"Either they need to hang that board lower, or you need to slow down," a voice behind her said.

"Right." She turned to catch a glimpse of Steve, a coworker, as she pushed her way into the sidewalk traffic.

"May I join you for lunch, or are you eating on the run again?"

"Yes, you can join me if you can catch me. I've gotta stop and buy three birthday cards on the way back. But actually, I do plan to sit down first. Burgers. Here, okay?" She gestured at the first patio café, and he pulled out chairs for both of them while she continued. "You'd think I'd get a little help at home. But no. Never. It's always *my* responsibility. Buy the gifts. Do the errands. Pick up the kids. Cook the meals. Call the parents. Clean the house. Decline the invitations. Balance the checkbook."

She sat down and burst into tears. Steve pulled his chair up beside her and looked concerned. "I'm sorry," she apologized. "It's just . . . a bad hair day." She tried to laugh it off.

"No, no," Steve countered, "definitely not a bad hair day." He leaned back and gave her an admiring glance. Then his voice grew more concerned. "No need to apologize. Listen, I've seen the pace you've been keeping lately. Just the hours here on this last project alone have been grueling. I hope your family appreciates what you're doing right now."

"Hmm, right," she snorted sarcastically. "Tyler is in his own world. All he cares about is his own research. And if he's awarded that grant next month, I'll see even less of him then than I do now—if that's possible. He has no idea what I do around the house to keep the family going. If he talks at all, it's to grumble about something I didn't do to suit him."

"That's too bad. Somebody needs to wake him up." Steve pushed back his chair. "Look, let me go order for us. You just sit here and relax a few minutes. At least I can give you ten minutes of peace and quiet. Then I'll be back with our food, and we'll talk it over."

Gratefully Shannon nodded as he headed off to stand in line. Just what she needed—someone who cared, someone ready to listen and offer help.

An affair waiting to happen.

Jorge Lopez turned out to be among the top ten salespeople in his organization after just twelve months on the job. It occurred to him that he might use his newly awarded President's Club credential as a stepping-stone to a better job with the leading company in the industry. He set up a meeting with his regional sales manager to discuss his potential for advancement in his company before deciding to look elsewhere.

"So after exceeding this year's sales goals by 20 percent, I just wanted to spend some time with you to discuss what you had in mind for my future here," Jorge said to his boss, Victor, over lunch.

"Bright. Very promising," Victor responded.

"That's good. But I guess I wanted to get a little clearer focus, a few more specific details."

"Why? We just recognized you with the President's Club award."

"I understand. And I appreciate that." Jorge waited, hoping he was taking the right approach. "But I . . . well, frankly, I've had a competitor approach me about going to work for them, and I just wanted to understand what my future here looks like."

His boss stiffened. "We don't play that game. You either like it here or you don't."

"Well, of course, I've enjoyed my work here. I just wanted to be able to compare what the future holds—apples to apples. I like what I do—I believe in our products, our prices, our policies, our people."

"Then I suggest you stay put. I don't have a crystal ball to predict the future. But one thing I can say for sure: Once you leave, you're out. We never rehire. We never look back. You make your decision; we make ours."

A resignation waiting to happen.

BUILDING SAFE HAVENS AND STRONG BONDS

We all need safe havens—places where we can go to feel safe emotionally, to be taken in and loved and appreciated for who we are, to find someone to share our accomplishments with and celebrate our successes, to enjoy a sense of belonging. We need it in our families, in our friendships, in our work. We *expect* it of our families. We *want* it from our friends. We *appreciate* it from our coworkers.

But the truth is that although we may *expect* it from our families, it doesn't just happen. To return to our movie metaphor, as creators of our life stories, we have to write those safe havens and strong relational bonds into the script before the actors get in front of the camera.

Madison discovers that she has to deal with her fears about her parents' relationship alone. Shannon feels "beat up" and ignored by her husband. Jorge discovers that he cannot express his goals and questions aloud to his boss without endangering his job.

Although you're not aiming for intimacy when you are writing scenes from your life story at work, you do need to connect with coworkers to elicit their cooperation and loyalty. Commonality builds camaraderie: common goals, common challenges, common commitments.

The worst part of success is to try to find someone who is
happy for you. —BETTE MIDLER

THE FIVE *Ts* OF SIGNATURE RELATIONSHIPS

In the same way you would structure a screenplay, you have
to create your life story to include scenes of connection long
before you need emotional support. Just as in the movies, these
emotional bonds deepen over time as you share the five *Ts*:
Time, Talk, Touch, Tough spots, and Tinsel.

Time

You have to spend time together if you want to build connection.
Our society went through an era of debating which was more
important in parenting: quality time or quantity time. The
correct answer? Both. We need to spend time with each other
as friends, parents, children, or teammates. Nothing creates
comfortableness around other people like time spent in their
presence, getting to know them—how they think, what they like
and don't like, what they value, what they find funny or not
funny, what makes them feel sad or significant. Strong bonds
are the result of our investment of time in our relationships.

Spending time with others, though, doesn't just "happen."
When the tasks on our to-do list cry out for attention, we tend
to give our energies to them. But building strong bonds is an
investment in the quality of the future relationship. If you have
difficulty thinking that far ahead, it may help to add "Spend
time with [spouse, son, daughter, grandparent, friend]" to your
to-do list for a while until your time investment becomes a
higher priority than the other tasks. The payoff will be worth
the effort.

Talk

The kind of honest, positive talk we looked at in the previous chapter builds intimacy. The dialogue between Katrina and Madison represented a mere exchange of words—a substitute for meaningful conversation. Two people build a free-flowing relationship only as both of them learn to talk and listen.

Opaque talk—talk that is indirect, misleading, nondisclosing, nonquestioning, or superficial—is squeezed from a strained relationship. Transparent talk—talk that is direct, honest, open, self-disclosing, questioning, and analytical—flows from a solid relationship and strengthens the relationship even more. Both types of talk—opaque and transparent—reflect the heart of the speaker and the quality of the relationship.

Touch

From birth, babies need human touch if they are to grow into emotionally healthy adults. Research studies abound on this issue. Ronald Barr, M.D., of the Child Development Program at Montreal Children's Hospital, found that increasing mother-baby contact reduces crying. Babies who are carried more cry less—especially at six weeks of age, when their tendency to cry is greatest. Tiffany Field, Ph.D., of the Touch Research Institute at the University of Miami School of Medicine, studied premature babies in the hospital's intensive care unit. Those who were massaged daily gained more weight, were more active, alert, and responsive, and were ready to go home an average of six days earlier than infants who did not receive daily massage.

Touch even decreases pain. Lewis Mehl-Madrona, M.D., Ph.D., and program director at the Center for Health and Healing at Beth Israel Medical Center in New York, reports that after a massage, a body's stress hormone levels drop and endorphins climb, which leads to a decreased perception of pain and an increased sense of well-being. That's why a parent's touch can soothe a crying child—even though the child may still be experiencing physical pain, the emotional satisfaction gained outweighs the pain of the skinned knee.

Touch continues to be vital at all ages. In another study at the University of Wisconsin-Eau Claire, researchers discovered that touch improved pain, tension, mood, satisfaction, and hand function in arthritic patients. The list of studies on the emotional and physical benefits of touch goes on and on.

Even as our training company coaches professional speakers in handling an audience, a key tactic in controlling hecklers or a hostile person or audience is to walk closer rather than withdraw. You want to get the other person to relate to you as another human being, not just as a speaker.

Families and friends who hug each other have a stronger chance of maintaining the same closeness emotionally. It's hard to hug someone you're not speaking to, so the pressure's on to talk out any difficulties before the next meet-and-greet, hug-or-huddle occasion.

Tough Spots

Facing tough spots and enduring adversity together build connection. Families who experience crises such as job loss, business disruption, major illness, or death, and face those challenges together, strengthen their bonds.

At work you build connections by facing the same challenges in less-than-desirable circumstances. You commiserate with each other through the highs and lows of various obstacles you encounter in the course of reaching your goals: surviving a merger without getting downsized or right-sized, experiencing a 25 percent salary cut for six months, speeding up production while losing staff. When you've survived the challenge, you gain a greater appreciation for each other's talents, attitudes, and commitments.

Whether the crisis involves family, friends, or coworkers, when it has passed, the intimacy that has developed through the shared struggle often remains.

Tough spots alone, however, are a difficult time to begin the bonding process. A huge financial setback or a job loss, for example, may break an already floundering marriage. A pending corporate layoff is a poor time to be trying to make amends with a boss or coworker. It's only when others of the five *Ts* are already present that this one can further cement the connection.

> *The love of our neighbor in all its fullness simply means*
> *being able to say to him, "What are you going through?"*
> —SIMONE WEIL

Tinsel

Tinsel refers to rituals related to a relationship, much the same way Christmas rituals connect us to memories of home. When we routinely eat popcorn and rent a movie with a certain friend, or regularly compete in golf tournaments with a best buddy, we build a connection by ritual in the same way that a couple thinks romantic thoughts when they hear "their" song. Here are some relationship rituals of the people we know:

- A grandfather takes his two grandsons to local pro football and baseball games.

- Six women drive out of state to a shopping mall for one weekend each year.
- Twelve couples play Dominoes 42 once a month at each other's homes—and have been doing so for the past twenty years.
- An extended family of fourteen goes on a two-week vacation together every summer.
- Two couples eat Sunday lunch together every week.
- Five coworkers meet for Bible study every Thursday morning before work.
- A mother and her daughters-in-law meet to give each other perms every three months.
- Two friends take continuing-education classes together every semester at a local university.

With coworkers, the tinsel rituals may be common commitments to a goal or a cause: to win the next proposal, to finish training twenty-five hundred employees on customer service, to design the highway system, to win the lawsuit, to solicit fifty million dollars in donated funds for a charity, to spearhead the blood drive each year.

Such rituals put pressure on us to solve differences and mend fences so that we can go back to "normal" in the relationship once we've reached our goal.

Do two walk together unless they have agreed to do so?

AMOS 3:3

These five *T*s will set the scene for characters to connect on a deeper, more intense level as they meet from occasion to occasion and crisis to crisis. The more of the five *T*s the characters share, generally the stronger their bond will be.

Adding the Finishing Touches to Your Blockbuster

In the movie scenario we looked at in the opening of this chapter, we don't wait for Kirk to get well so that he and Jason can become good friends, go to the ball field together, and discuss Kirk's marriage problems. All the minor scenes of connection come *before* the climax when Jason must decide to donate the kidney even if it means losing his job and endangering his own life.

The same is true with your own signature relationships. You need to create chemistry so that you and your other "cast members" get along on the set before a crisis occurs. Work to build strong bonds. Then on days of torrential downpours, the rains won't affect the turnout at your box office.

> *Familiarity, truly cultivated, can breed love.*
> —DR. JOYCE BROTHERS

> *A cord of three strands is not quickly broken.*
> —ECCLESIASTES 4:12

> *Love is a choice—not simply, or necessarily, a rational choice, but rather a willingness to be present to others without pretense or guile.*   —CARTER HEYWARD

ELEVEN

FLASHBACKS AND FORESHADOWING
Forgiving the Future

*I*s there someone you haven't forgiven?

*I*s resentment damaging your own personality?

THE SCHOOL bus dropped Chris Carrier at the corner near his house about noon after his early release from school for the Christmas holidays. The Florida sunshine promised a beautiful afternoon of play with his friends. He looked up when he heard a man's voice: "You must be Hugh Carrier's boy; you look just like him." The man explained that he worked for Chris's father and was decorating for a surprise party and needed his help. The year was 1974—long before children and parents received daily warnings on the television about abductions.

Chris walked with the man back down the street to the man's nearby motor home, and they headed out of town. After a while the man handed Chris a map and told him to look for a certain road while he got something out of the back.

Chris thought he felt a bee sting on his left shoulder. He turned to swat it—and discovered the man standing beside him with an ice pick. He yanked Chris from his seat, dropped him onto the floor of the motor home, and began to stab him repeatedly in the chest with the ice pick, leaving only shallow half-inch cuts.

Then the man drove him to Turner River Road, a sparsely populated area, and left him a little way from the property-line fence post, telling him his dad would pick him up shortly. Chris was relieved. He would be safe now. His dad would be picking him up any minute.

When Chris turned his head in the opposite direction, he felt a small revolver against his temple. The man pulled the trigger, blinding Chris, and left him for dead at dusk on December 20.

Six days later Chris's dad called the family together. As a successful lawyer, he had called in all the favors owed him from law enforcement agencies to put more staff on the case. The reward money he'd put up had brought in no results. He cried out to God, "I've done all I can do; now it's up to you."

About two hours later, Chris woke up from his six-day nap in the Everglades. He'd lived without protection from the weather or wild animals—except for God's hand. In that remote area he might have sat on the rock next to the road for days—or until he starved—before anyone came by. But a man on a hunting trip with his two children drove by and found him.

It was only as doctors tried to discover why Chris couldn't see that a diagnostic test revealed the path of the bullet through his head. Fear became a steady companion in the days that followed as the authorities tried to track his abductor.

From Chris's description, the authorities arrested a suspect,

whom Chris's father and uncle identified as a man they had hired
to care for a great-uncle who had suffered a stroke. The man was
fired after six months. Police went to David McAllister's motor
home and found a gun of the caliber used to shoot Chris. But
Chris couldn't identify him positively, and the authorities lacked
the necessary forensics evidence to take him to trial.

For twenty-two years Chris lived with the trauma and without
his eyesight. Then a police officer who had worked on the case
discovered David McAllister in a nursing home, bedridden, blind
from glaucoma, and near death. The officer told him that he
was no longer in danger of punishment and encouraged him
to confess to the crime so the family could have closure.

When the officer called Chris to ask if he'd like to talk to the
man who had left him in the woods for dead, Chris definitely
wanted to face his abductor. The man had stabbed him repeatedly with an ice pick. The man had shot him in the temple.
The man had abandoned him and left him for dead in the
Everglades.

When Chris walked into McAllister's room in the nursing
home, the man was evasive at first but then confessed to all of it.

Chris's reaction? Immediate forgiveness. How could he not
forgive? How could he not see God's hand of protection
through the entire ordeal? Stabbed in the chest repeatedly,
but he did not die? Shot in the temple at point-blank range, but
he did not die? Left in the Everglades in the winter among wild
animals for six days, but he did not die? Awake and sitting on
a rock in an isolated spot just when a hunter passed by?

Chris remained in Florida, visiting his abductor five times
in the next six days, each time explaining that the basis of his
forgiveness was his relationship with Jesus Christ and that he

wished their newfound friendship to extend beyond this life. He encouraged David McAllister to discard his load of guilt and to understand that Chris had much to be grateful for—a good education, a wonderful marriage, and two loving daughters.

David McAllister accepted God's forgiveness and gift of eternal life—and died three weeks later.

Chris's story of forgiveness has had far-reaching influence as he has told the story repeatedly on national media and as he teaches at San Marcos Baptist Academy. His ministry involves helping youth deal with anger about situations they can't control and don't understand.

> *What the church needs today are more calloused hands*
> *and fewer calloused hearts.*   —UNKNOWN

AN UNNATURAL ACT

Chris's story made national headlines—not solely because of the abduction but because of its unusual ending. Forgiveness is unnatural in such circumstances. But having known Chris's wife since her childhood, I can attest to the fact that Chris comes from a long line of forgivers and also married into such a family. This kind of mind-set is both taught and caught.

The unforgiving spirit so prevalent in America has been the subject of more than one political commentator and religious leader: "Here [in America] we write well when we expose frauds and hypocrites. We are great at counting warts and blemishes and weighing feet of clay. In expressing love, we belong among the undeveloped countries," observed novelist Saul Bellow.

It's true not only of those in public life; it's doubly true
of those who offend us personally. Where forgiveness is the issue,
sometimes it seems the closer the relationship, the deeper the
wound, the longer the grudge. How can this be? Shouldn't we
be most eager to forgive those closest to us? Why do we find it
so hard to forgive family members?

First, because we tend to personalize everything about
them as they relate to us. Everyone slips up occasionally. These
offenses are often just random acts of thoughtlessness or insen-
sitivity—not intentional insults—but because they come from
those closest to us, we categorize them as personal affronts.
We promptly assign intentions and motives to the offender.

Second, we are wounded deeply precisely because the offenders are our closest friends and family supporters. When they
do something thoughtless or hurtful, we feel double the pain
because we care more about what they think or feel than we do
about what others think or feel.

If a committee member implies that we're irresponsible, we
may not mind all that much, perhaps because we don't really
value his opinion or because we won't miss his association with
us if he withdraws it. But if our best friend says we're irresponsible, we value her opinion, question our own behavior that would
cause her to make such a judgment, and miss the relationship if
she withdraws.

Third, we tend to hold grudges because we feel safe in the
relationship. The other people have to love us anyway—after
all, they're our father or sister or spouse. Besides, grudges can
come in handy; we like to "trade" forgiveness for favors. The
thinking goes like this: "You wounded me. I now can hold a
grudge against you, and you need me to forgive you. When I

want something from you, I'll trade you forgiveness in exchange for the favor."

Some people hang on to an offense the way a police officer carries a pair of handcuffs. They think that as long as they refuse to forgive, the offender is chained to them. Not so. The officer wearing the empty handcuffs on his belt doesn't keep them from swinging freely, but they may limit the officer's freedom of movement. In the same way, when we hold a grudge, we don't necessarily imprison the one who wronged us, but carrying the grudge can drain emotional energy and limit our freedom.

Offenders are not held in check by our grudges or resentment. To give up that resentment is not to free them. They are free already—maybe not to associate with us but to associate with others and to go on with their life. When we forgive others, we free *ourselves*. An unforgiving person becomes a complaining, grumbling, whining person who repels others. Forgiving others releases us from such bitterness. It heals our personalities and permits peace of mind.

> If you have a thing to pardon, pardon it quickly. Slow forgiveness is little better than no forgiveness.
>
> —ARTHUR W. PINERO

When I think of some of the offenses in my life, my mind quickly goes to those who've experienced far worse situations for which they've had to find the strength to forgive: those who have experienced child abuse, spousal abuse, the murder of a child. Some have had to find a way to forgive these offenders and continue the relationship. Only God can provide the strength to offer forgiveness in such relationships and situations.

Forgiveness is an act of the will, and the will can function regardless of the temperature of the heart.

—CORRIE TEN BOOM

THE GUILTY HANG BY A THREAD

There *is* an exception to the earlier statement that when you have an unforgiving spirit it imprisons only you. Your lack of forgiveness *can* imprison those who feel guilty about something they did or didn't do to you. Guilt binds people together in strange ways. Those wronged can leverage money, attention, time, and good deeds from people who feel guilty about past offenses.

But feelings of guilt rarely generate love and intimacy. As long as the offended plays "poor me," the relationship between offended and offender hangs by a thread. Only when those offended offer forgiveness and a clean slate can they move on toward a future that holds promise for a stronger connection.

People who fight fire with fire usually end up with ashes.

—ABIGAIL VAN BUREN

Do You Really Want to Keep Score?

The credit card clerk messes up your monthly statement, causing you grief, but she apologizes profusely and corrects it. You get over it. Strangers stand out of sight and out of mind. You don't have to relate to them every day at the coffeemaker or committee meeting.

But that's precisely the point. Sometimes a difficulty in "relating" after an offending incident can be a true test of whether real forgiveness has occurred.

Hating people is like burning down your own house to get rid of a rat.   —HARRY EMERSON FOSDICK

When creating your life story, if you decide to save and monitor the wrongs rather than delete them as they happen, you end up "keeping score." Your mental scorecard may look something like this:

He Offended	I Forgave	Offenses—My Dad	I Offended	He Forgave
X		Always sent child support check late—must have resented me		
X		Didn't ask my opinion about trip		
X	X	Didn't visit when we invited him		
X		Never thanks me for calling		
		Never thank him for calling me	X	?
X		Doesn't take an interest in my job		
X	X	Can't remember the kids' hobbies		
Result: He owes me.				

He Offended	I Forgave	Offenses—Coworker Jesse	I Offended	He Forgave
X		Withheld key information from me		
X		Excludes me in networking with VIPs		
X		Took credit for my ideas for saving money		
X		Didn't back me in conflict with the boss		
		Withheld key information from him	X	X
X		Never offers to help when I have a crunch deadline on a key project even though I help him out often		
Result: He owes me.				

She Offended	I Forgave	Offenses—Sarah	I Offended	She Forgave
X	X	Never told me how much she paid for the family farm		
		Never told her that she sings well, and I know she needs that praise from me	X	
X	X	Never offered to help take care of Grandmother when she was sick		
X	X	Is so self-centered that she never asks the rest of the family what we'd like to do		
X	X	Lets her kids misbehave and show disrespect to me and mistreat my kids		
X	X	Brags about her husband's achievements and implies that they're better off than we are		
Result: She owes me.				

When considering all your relationships over the span of a decade or two or three, it may become a little difficult to keep things straight. Who's up and who's down? Who owes whom what, when, why? Are you sure? Would God agree?

Although we probably keep a separate scorecard for each of our relationships, my guess is that God keeps all our scores on one screen.

Life is too short for keeping scorecards. Ask yourself, Do I really want to push the "pause" button on a relationship, or do I want to keep these people as characters in my life story?

> If you forgive those who sin against you, your heavenly
> Father will forgive you.   MATTHEW 6:14, NLT

Interactions with All Other People in Your Life—God's Perspective	Yes	No	Need God's Forgiveness
Did you lose your temper with anyone today?	X		X
Have you ever been jealous?	X		X
Did you apologize to Jesse yet for your withdrawal and ill will because of jealousy?		X	X
Have you lied today?	X		X
Did you mislead Sarah last week?	X		X
Did you put self-interest above another person's interest today in the meeting?	X		X
Did you speak harshly to someone today?	X		X
Have you failed to show concern for others today?	X		X
Have you been unkind or thoughtless to anyone today?	X		X
Are you still being unkind to your dad when he calls?	X		X
Have you been disloyal to either Jesse, your boss, your assistant, or your client today?	X		X
Results: Asked for Forgiveness Today? **Didn't Ask for Forgiveness Today?**			

It is very easy to forgive others their mistakes; it takes more grit and gumption to forgive them for having witnessed your own.

—JESSAMYN WEST

Adding the Finishing Touches to Your Blockbuster

Whether drama or comedy, a good story always involves conflict: Boy meets girl. Boy loses girl. Boy wins girl. Where there's conflict between the two main characters, typically somebody gets wounded. Then the offended forgives the offender instead of just forgetting the offense. But the movie or novel never ends with the forgiveness scene. There's always one final scene to show that the two characters have *really* forgiven each other—in deed, not just in word.

Successful relationships in real life follow the same plotline. No matter who "wins" during a conflict, both people involved have to forgive before they can move on. Not to do so is to hit the "pause" button on their own lives.

You've heard it said, "Forgive and forget the past." That's not possible. The past pops into memory all too easily. But you can decide to forgive the future—you can free the other person to continue composing a new scene with you on a clean screen. You can make a conscious effort to "edit" the offense from your life story and continue unencumbered in the relationship. That's what God does for each of us every day.

> *Write injuries in dust, benefits in marble.*   —FRENCH PROVERB

> *If men wound you with injuries, meet them with patience; hasty words rankle the wound, soft language dresses it, forgiveness cures it, and oblivion takes away the scar.*
>   —FRANCIS BEAUMONT

> *Be patient with each other, making allowance for each other's faults because of your love.*   —EPHESIANS 4:2, NLT

TWELVE

STARRING ROLES
Striving to Serve—Even If You're the Star

*W*hy will others miss you when you're gone?

*H*ow do you demonstrate true humility?

CHRISTMAS mornings meant a bonanza for my brother, my sister, and me. But I remember that after flying into my pile of gifts, I always looked meekly at the one to three small gifts for Mother and Dad. One gift if we three kids had pooled our money and bought them something "big," relatively speaking. Three, if we individually had squeezed a few dollars out of our allowances to buy them a gift.

In any case, I remember feeling a twinge of guilt that Mom and Dad received so few gifts themselves, and I thought it must be sad to be the parents at Christmastime. When I expressed that thought once when I was about eight, Mom and Dad just laughed and quoted the verse "It is more blessed to give than to receive" (Acts 20:35). I could never quite understand that as a child. Of course, now that I've had children of my own, I understand completely.

But the concept of giving by serving proves harder to understand.

THE BIG ROLE REVERSAL

The world's idea of greatness is to have others give to you or serve you. The president has advisors, aides, and ambassadors. Generals have first lieutenants, captains, and majors. Movie stars have press agents, money managers, and make-up artists. CEOs have administrative assistants, chauffeurs, and pilots. Land barons have real estate agents, accountants, and tax advisors. Professional athletes have coaches, personal trainers, and physical therapists. Professors have researchers, media specialists, and teaching assistants.

> *The true measure of a man is not the number of servants he has, but the number of people he serves.* —ARNOLD GLASOW

It's not that these people don't need assistants; it's just that we tend to attach the idea of greatness to the idea of being served. The Bible, however, presents the opposite view: "The greatest among you will be your servant" (Matthew 23:11). Jesus Christ himself lived a life of service. He spent three years healing the sick, cooking breakfast on the beach for his disciples, washing their feet, and teaching them how to live with each other and settle their disputes.

The biggest problem with linking greatness to being served is making this next leap in logic: If people around us care about us, they should serve us to demonstrate their devotion. It follows, then, that if my spouse loves me, he/she will do whatever I ask, spend money on what I want, live where I want to live, spend time with me whenever I say so, and generally subordinate his/her wishes to mine.

If my children love me, they'll do my errands for me, please me in their choice of friends, marry whomever I approve, choose the college I prefer, select the vocation I think best, come home for the holidays when I want them to, and take care of my needs whenever I call.

If my friends appreciate me, they'll listen whenever I need to talk, come over when I ask, go with me when I invite them, lend me money when I need it, and do whatever personal favors I need.

If my work colleagues admire me, they'll support me on controversial issues in group situations, cover for my mistakes, do whatever I say without question, and take on the tasks I don't enjoy doing myself.

When spouses, children, friends, and coworkers don't respond this way, we feel upset and consider the relationship to be in danger. If you want to improve the scenes in your blockbuster life story, maybe you need a role reversal: consider being the one who serves.

There are three reasons for this role reversal: (1) God commands us to serve others, (2) serving benefits others through our generous actions, and (3) serving others builds character in us—it creates humility. Because God created us and commanded us to serve, obviously he had in mind our doing his work in the world as his hands and feet. And no one would argue that service to others is a good thing. Almost everyone has good intentions, even if they lack the discipline to follow through on them.

But because the focus here is on relationships, let's zero in on the third reason for serving others—building character, specifically, humility. Now that's something almost everyone has to work on writing into their life scripts.

The value of a man resides in what he gives and not in what he is capable of receiving.   —ALBERT EINSTEIN

SERVING OTHERS BUILDS CHARACTER

You may have heard about a fictitious book titled *Humility and How I Attained It.* We laugh at the idea because we know that if you have to *tell* someone you're humble, you're not. Humility that calls attention to itself is false humility.

But true humility lays the foundation for service in all of our relationships, so you may want to consider developing that quality in the central character of your life story, no matter what plotline you eventually develop.

What does true humility look like? It does not insist on having its own way. It looks out for the best interest of the other person in the relationship. Humility entertains the idea that someone else just might be right—and you just might be wrong. Humility can apologize for a situation—even when your action itself is not wrong. Humility does not always consider rank or position as the ultimate criteria in deciding who should do a specific task. Humility does not feel jealous when others receive praise; instead, it can be happy when others receive honors and recognition.

Have you heard admirers of celebrities and other important people make comments such as these: "He seems so down-to-earth." "She never puts on airs." "They made me feel so comfortable." "He walked to the park just like the rest of us—no special hoopla." "During the discussion he never even mentioned his title—somebody else told me after it was all over." "She gave me her coat when I said it was cold—I didn't know she was the owner of the place."

Chances are great that family, friends, and coworkers will not remember main characters fondly for their pride, strong will, or demands to be served. Instead, they will be more likely to remember them for the words and actions that made those around them feel important. Let's look at some of the circumstances and arenas in which we may find ourselves as we strive to serve.

Humility is illusive. It is such a fragile plant that the slightest reference to it causes it to wilt and die.   —UNKNOWN

Do nothing from selfishness or empty conceit, but with humility of mind let each of you regard one another as more important than himself; do not merely look out for your own personal interests, but also for the interests of others.
    —PHILIPPIANS 2:3-4, NASB

Do not think of yourself more highly than you ought.
    —ROMANS 12:3

Whoever exalts himself will be humbled, and whoever humbles himself will be exalted.   —MATTHEW 23:12

Serving in the Spotlight
Just like the song "Looking for Love in All the Wrong Places," some people are looking to serve in all the wrong places. They

seek out spotlight situations that guarantee them praise, promotion, or practice for other more profitable pursuits. These opportunities for service go fast. Volunteers stand in line waiting their turn.

For example, many are willing to act as honorary chairpersons for fund-raising efforts and as honorary directors and board members of nonprofit organizations. Their celebrity names bring attention to the cause, goal, or foundation. Some organizations appoint staff members to serve in charity drives for the PR value and goodwill such efforts generate in the community. Salespeople may serve on committees for good causes as a way to meet clients. Parents may volunteer to serve in a parent-teacher organization because it can be a stepping-stone on the way to a larger political goal. Soloists may serve in worship services because of the personal praise they receive.

Granted, all of these roles of service are vital. They provide great benefit to others. And God alone knows the motives of people's hearts. But could it be that too many of us have learned to serve only in the spotlight and that those spotlight situations don't surface often enough to prepare us for serving in every-day relationships? The question we need to raise is this: What do we understand of service when the spotlight is off?

"Who has not served cannot command," observed Italian writer and translator John Florio (ca. 1553–1625). That could explain the reason we have such a huge demand for leadership training in the country today. In corporations, in government agencies, and in the military, leadership frequently tops the list of most requested speech and course topics and continues to be a hot commodity. Those who have not served when the spotlight is off are unprepared to lead when the spotlight is on.

Serving in Conflict

While many people are eager to serve in the spotlight, other opportunities for service go begging. One of the best times to serve others is when we feel like it the least—when there's a conflict. The Bible puts it like this: "If someone forces you to go one mile, go with him two miles" (Matthew 5:41). Go above and beyond duty and expectation—especially when there's a squabble. Nothing demonstrates goodwill in a relationship like giving *more* service than what someone has demanded of you.

If your manager demands that you work until midnight on Thursday to get a project completed, volunteer to work over the weekend to get another project started, and see how the relationship changes for the better.

If your spouse asks you to change your vacation preferences and go together to his or her favorite destination instead, agree willingly. Help with the travel arrangements. Don't ask for reciprocation the following year, and see how the relationship changes for the better.

If your sister-in-law insists that Thanksgiving festivities be at her house this year so the holidays will be easier on her and her family and they don't have to travel, ask if you can help with the meal. See how the relationship changes for the better.

Of course, this is not to suggest that you become a "doormat" and routinely do everything another person demands just to keep peace in a relationship. But it is to say that serving can be a conscious choice in responding to sporadic conflict.

Consider conflict a chance to go the extra mile and create a more pleasant scene.

Service is the rent that we pay for our room on earth.

—LORD HALIFAX

Serving Uphill in the Hot Seat

Occasionally you may have an opportunity to serve in challenging roles that produce dramatic results and benefit many people. Maybe you're asked to mediate a conflict among a group setting policy on major issues in the community, and nobody else will take the job because of the potential for making enemies.

Or perhaps you've been asked to raise funds for a worthy cause—and there's no publicity attached. The effort involves your credibility in calling in personal favors for the benefit of the cause.

Maybe you've been asked to serve in government to help pass important legislation or to "fight city hall" to ensure fair treatment for certain groups of people.

Such service may prove difficult for any number of reasons, but an uphill challenge makes the results of your service even more memorable to those who receive the benefit from your willingess to take on a "thankless" task.

It is when we forget ourselves that we do things that are likely to be remembered.   —UNKNOWN

Serving in Your Sweats

Sometimes serving in your sweats can be the most difficult of all—that is, serving in routine ways in ordinary situations. There is no applause. There are no photo ops. And there are no dramatic results for a great number of people. But these may be the best opportunities for you to build the trait of humility into the leading character in your blockbuster.

Maybe the service involves something physically difficult, such as moving your elderly neighbor or relative into a new apartment. The work involves back-breaking lifting, scrubbing and cleaning, painting, and making repairs—things you might even pay someone else to do if you had to make the move yourself. But when you learn to serve in your sweats, you do these things yourself to serve the other person—and you tell no one.

> *It is not where you serve, but how you serve.*
>
> —J. RUBIN CLARK

> *Your attitude should be the same as that of Christ Jesus . . . [who took on] the very nature of a servant.*
>
> —PHILIPPIANS 2:5-7

Dan Weedon, a friend of ours, serves in his sweats three to four days a week. Having taken early retirement from his job as a research chemist, he now spends his time serving his friends, members of his church, and others in the community. For example, in a recent week he helped a widow move into a new apartment and trimmed branches from the trees blocking the view on the farm of an elderly neighbor—a project he has been working on "a few trees a week" for the past several months. He drove two senior citizens to their doctor appointments. He drove an elderly church member to chemotherapy and stayed with her for three hours because she was afraid. Saturday he spent mowing lawns as a supervisor to youth on work assignment under probation in the juvenile court system. That was one week of service—a rather typical week.

My own dad's weeks are similar. Although he has had a servant's heart all his life, now at age seventy-seven and after a couple of heart attacks in the last twenty years, he has had to slow down a bit. His typical month of volunteer service looks something like this: He's on the committee to help count the Sunday offerings every Monday morning at the church. He and my mom volunteered one afternoon a week to greet weekday visitors to the church while the facilities were under construction and all signs were down. They visit those in their age group who are hospitalized—and that sometimes means three or four visits per week, waiting with families through long surgeries. Once a month they cook and serve a meal in the city's homeless shelter and get the guests ready for the night. He plays jack-of-all-trades for a neighborhood widow—doing anything from changing lightbulbs to hauling away discarded magazines to cleaning out the gutters. When he was younger, his weekly service list was much longer.

> *To devote a portion of one's leisure to doing something for someone else is one of the highest forms of recreation.*
> —GERALD B. FITZGERALD

> *Show me your faith without deeds, and I will show you my faith by what I do.*
> —JAMES 2:18

My granddad and grandmother Daniels also served in sweats. For most of Granddad's life, he worked in the salt mines of east Texas and grew vegetables on a truck farm on the side.

My grandparents worked as a team to serve their friends and family. He farmed and harvested the vegetables and brought them to the house for Grandmother to can or freeze. When they had "put up" all they could eat, they bought a second freezer to store the rest so they'd have enough to give away to others in need. Had they delivered all the goodies to one family rather than to ten or twelve, it would have been enough to feed a family of six for a year.

On Sundays they served again. Granddad always made three trips to church, transporting all the widows who didn't own cars or could no longer drive. Not many days went by that he and my mother didn't visit the sick in the hospital.

In their marriage, the pattern was the same. My granddad showed his love to my grandmother by serving her. Although they both worked hard on the farm and in the salt mines, he washed as many dishes as she did. He cooked as many meals as she did. He bought groceries more often than she did. He mopped the floor as often as she did. He washed the clothes as often as she did. And when she was sick the last few years of her life, he waited on her hand and foot until her death.

For sixty-four years, he served her because he loved her.

Serve one another in love.   —GALATIANS 5:13

Adding the Finishing Touches to Your Blockbuster

Neither moviegoers nor novel readers like cocky stars. There may be scenes, of course, where we hear braggadocio from the heroes or heroines. But overall, the novelist or screenwriter lets us know that arrogance is not the character's true nature. In fact, in real life if the media begins to report occasions when a star haughtily scorns fans, the star's popularity often plummets.

Audiences and readers demand a level of humility in their stars, but the novelists and scriptwriters themselves also assume a role of service. Even though they may play "god" in the sense that they create the characters and their destiny, they also serve—the editor, the producer, the talk-show host, and ultimately their audiences.

In theater, the roles of characters who demand to be served can often be played by understudies. After all, they have only a few lines of dialogue—making requests or demands or giving orders. The real work or acting comes from those performing the service.

The same situation exists in our personal relationships. Those who demand to be served do so because of pride. People tend to cherish most those who serve them. When you write your life story, if you want to ensure that others will miss you when you're not in the scene anymore, make your character a person who serves others.

> *No man was ever honored for what he received; honor has been the reward for what he gave.*   —CALVIN COOLIDGE

> *Our true destiny is not to be ministered unto but to minister to ourselves and to our fellow men.*
> —FRANKLIN DELANO ROOSEVELT

> *Let your light shine before men, that they may see your good deeds and praise your Father in heaven.*   —MATTHEW 5:16

THIRTEEN

PACING AND COMIC RELIEF

*Laughing to Lighten the Load, Lengthen Your Days,
and Infect Others*

*W*hy do you think you miss the point of jokes and funny remarks?

*D*oes your humor ever sting?

"I CAN'T do it!" I yelled to my husband over the roaring motor as we bounced at full speed over the waves. "I can swim. I can dive. I can float on my back all day long. I just can't ski."

"Sure you can," he yelled back in his declarative, what-more-needs-to-be-said tone.

"I can't."

"Yes, you can."

"I can't. I've tried it. I don't have enough strength in my arms. The rope pulls right out of my hand." I glanced over at daughter Lisa to demonstrate the way the rope always jerks me like a puppet and then leaves me to splash face first into the froth.

"You just need somebody who knows what they're talking about to work with you," my husband urged.

"I've tried to ski since I was sixteen. And I've had plenty of people trying to teach me. I can't even lift my feet up to keep my skis parallel."

Vernon cut the engine, and the boat stopped suddenly. Lisa, already in her life jacket, tossed her inner tube into the water and then jumped into the center of it to sun herself.

"You *can* ski if you make up your mind to," my husband said to me and turned to occupy himself with something under the dash. I climbed down the ladder and paddled out in the water.

I treaded water for a few minutes, expecting him to join me in the water for the "lesson," which I wasn't particularly eager to have. When he didn't follow me down the ladder, I snapped, "Well, are you coming? I'm not going to stay out here in the middle of the lake all day. Alone."

Lisa swirled her inner tube around and popped off, "So what am I—a buoy?"

We cracked up. Immediately the tenor of the conversation changed. Such is the value of humor. There is a right time for everything. A time to laugh, a time to cry. Fortunately, humor fits most occasions and most relationships.

Humor is like a needle and thread—deftly used it can patch up just about everything.   —UNKNOWN

DO YOU GET IT? YOU DO GET IT, DON'T YOU?

Well-adjusted people have a healthy sense of humor. They find it easy to laugh. That doesn't necessarily mean they're pranksters or great storytellers; it means they see the bright side of life.

They see ironies and humorous incidents in the ordinary circumstances and happenings of everyday life. They can laugh at the foibles of humanity in general and at their own weaknesses specifically. The ability to laugh is like a safety valve; when tension gets high, laughter helps you let off steam so you don't blow your stack under pressure.

To make mistakes is human; to stumble is commonplace; to be able to laugh at yourself is maturity.

—WILLIAM ARTHUR WARD

Less well-adjusted people tend to be short a funny bone or two. They fail to see humor in everyday happenings. When they hear others wisecrack, they often don't catch the joke and tend to miss the point of funny stories that people tell about their escapades. For them, life is too serious to "waste" on laughing. They just don't get it.

Humor lengthens our days. Long ago the writer of the book of Proverbs stated, "A merry heart does good, like medicine" (Proverbs 17:22, NKJV). Current research studies now support that biblical statement and document many benefits of having a well-developed sense of humor. The sections that follow look at three of these benefits.

Laughter is God's hand on a troubled world.   —UNKNOWN

Humor Helps Us Bear the Unpleasant

A principal of a local high school faced one of the most challenging discussions educators must handle when he had to call the parents of one his students. Their son had been dealing drugs on campus. Toward the end of a very stressful session with the parents, whose emotions had ranged from anger to defensiveness to guilt to embarrassment to hurt, the principal ended on a positive note with this comment: "Well, it's obvious your son has natural sales skills. We just need to find him a better product."

His ability to use humor to lighten a very heavy load for the parents made this unpleasant discussion bearable.

Illness is another unpleasant circumstance where humor packs a powerful punch. My friend Kim Collins has been dealing with cancer for the past two years. It seems that every kind of complication that can accompany cancer and its treatment has been part of her ordeal. And she has met it all with her typical good humor, often putting at ease her friends and family who didn't know what to say and how to say it at the onslaught of various predicaments. One-liners have become her forte during recuperation. In fact, she's so witty that her friends have told her she's one of the few people who *can* give up her day job.

In times of serious conflict such as war, people need humor all the more. Attendance at comedy movies increases. Even on the battlefield, surrounded by death, soldiers use humor to ease their tension. A prime example would be this sign above a fox-hole: "Holiday Inn Resort—Maximum Occupancy 16. In case of incoming strike, 160."

As you and your family face financial crises, health concerns, child-rearing dilemmas, or in-law misunderstandings, focus on human foibles for a laugh. As you and team members or a supervisor get crossways on a project and the tension mounts, look for a lighthearted moment that will allow everyone to let off steam.

No matter how serious or trivial the situation—have you ever driven cross-country with two toddlers in rainy weather?—humor helps lighten the load and helps us to see people and problems from a proper perspective.

Humor Helps Us Cope with Surprises

Several years back we invited sixty guests to a party at our house. We were serving an exotic "theme" meal from India that included hot chicken curry over rice and various condiments such as peanuts, pineapple, coconut, and so forth. In preparing the food, I plugged in eight Crock-Pots simultaneously to reheat the curry sauce—and plunged the whole house into total darkness. Obviously we'd blown a circuit. We flipped the breaker switch and tried again. Lights on. Lights off. We flipped the switch and tried again. Lights on. Lights off.

A house full of company in total darkness with cold curry. Dealing with the unexpected can introduce tension in a marriage—with or without the cold curry. So the guests began to entertain themselves, lobbing one-liners back and forth for a good twenty minutes until an electrician got the power back on.

Humor generally spreads until it "infects" others and alters everyone's mood. Even one lighthearted person in a relationship of two can change things. Two or three individuals with a sense of humor in a work group of six or seven can bring on an epidemic—and create a change in atmosphere so widespread that you can't quarantine it.

A man without mirth is like a wagon without springs; he is jolted disagreeably by every pebble in the road.

—HENRY WARD BEECHER

Humor Helps Us Overlook the Unattractive

The first day I walked into Miss Amos's American literature class, I was scared. Not because of the subject or the fact that this was my first day in a new school in a new class of 465 students in a new city. I was frightened by her face. Her nose was, well, huge and curved sharply toward the left cheekbone. Big dark bags hung under piercing dark eyes. Her cheeks were sunk in and then exploded into an oddly shaped, oversized mouth. Her silver hair gave evidence that she had paid some serious attention to her appearance. It was parted perfectly straight and combed flat down to her ears, then held in place by a tight roll of pin curls around the edges. Below her neck, everything else seemed normal, wrapped in a smartly tailored dress. But her face—I couldn't take my eyes off her face.

I took my seat and slid around to look at her squarely. In big bold print she silently wrote *MISS AMOS* on the chalkboard behind her. Then turning to face us, she said, "You'll notice there's no period after the *Miss*—that makes it all too final. I'm still hoping."

The class laughed uneasily, and that began my junior year with Miss Amos.

By the third week in September, her bulletin board was completely outlined with white homecoming mums and green ribbons, each sprouting a glittering number in the center. Two days before the homecoming game, the bulletin board had mums three rows deep inside the flowered frame. Her explanation? Former students had sent them "just because."

In October a burly football player sauntered into class late, mumbling apologies about oversleeping. Miss Amos harrumphed and said, "Chris, if you're sleeping more than three hours a night, you're sleeping your life away. At age eighteen do you know how much of your life you've already missed?" He slid into his seat sheepishly. But as she surveyed the room with her sardonic stare, the comment was not lost on the rest of us. (Nor, apparently, was it lost on Chris, for that matter. He's now a state senator.)

Miss Amos taught us to manage time, to research, to speak, to write, and to think. I'm still drawing from the well she dug in my life—mostly through the use of homespun humor wrapped around a heart of love.

By May, I hardly noticed her face anymore. I guess most other students forgot about it also. The twenty to thirty homecoming mums kept arriving every football season, and later Miss Amos had a school named after her.

Humor hides a multitude of unattractive physical features, petty habits, and personality quirks that might otherwise irritate us. For example, you may have coworkers or relatives that you've helped and helped and helped—and they have the unattractive habit of being ungrateful. They never acknowledge your help or say thank you. You may be associated with a group of people at work, in your neighborhood, in your community, or in your church who have the unattractive quirk of never contributing to the effort. They "sponge" off everyone else—for food, for gas, even for entertainment.

When dealing with the unattractive, you have a choice—to get upset or to get a laugh. Getting upset boosts your blood pressure; laughing just gives you a boost.

Good humor is one of the best articles of dress one can wear in society.
—WILLIAM MAKEPEACE THACKERAY

THE HUMOR HANDBOOK

Humor rises to the surface in any number of ways: listening to fun music, taking a lighthearted approach to solving problems, finding the positive in the negative situation. So how do you draft your humor handbook so that you can respond in a lighthearted rather than a heavy-handed way to tension in relationships?

First, learn to laugh at yourself. Understand that your reputation, ego, career, future, or love is not on the line with every mistake, decision, circumstance, or situation that develops. Practice a little self-deprecating humor—admit a few mistakes, errors in judgment, or wrong decisions by telling funny stories on yourself. You'll likely see that others' opinions of you don't fall. In fact, their esteem and admiration will likely grow because of your willingness to be vulnerable with them about your own foibles. If you come across as less than perfect, they will feel that they have more in common with you because of their own shortcomings.

Second, give others permission to laugh at your mistakes without malice. When someone cracks a joke or delivers a one-liner at your expense, rather than be defensive, enjoy the humor yourself. Others take their cue from you. Assume no malice or ill will on the part of others until it is proved beyond a shadow of doubt that they actually meant to hurt or embarrass you. (When that's the case, you'll want to talk with them privately about the underlying cause for their hurtful humor.)

Finally, remember to test your own motives in directing humor toward others. Genuine humor holds humanity as a whole up for inspection but leaves no sting. Never disguise a "message" to someone in a humorous barb. Humor should strengthen and heal, not hurt, our relationships.

A man shows his character by what he laughs at.

—GERMAN PROVERB

True humor springs not more from the head than from the heart. It is not contempt; its essence is love. It issues not in laughter, but in still smiles, which lie far deeper.

—THOMAS CARLYLE

Adding the Finishing Touches to Your Blockbuster

The top fifty all-time biggest box-office hits include far more dramas than comedies. But even in drama, screenwriters introduce lines of comic relief to reduce tension. Novelists, too, know the importance of pacing for readers: two dramatic action scenes, followed by a lighter scene, and then a return to the action.

If we divided our real life into dramatic and comic scenes, drama would probably dominate. So our everyday lives, too, call for pacing. Humor helps ease the tension in relationships and situations so that we can work through difficulties in a more relaxed and receptive frame of mind.

As you write your own blockbuster life story, don't forget to set the proper mood theme music and setting and to balance the interaction between characters with humor. When the action gets hectic and the tension builds, slow the pace with some lighter scenes and humorous dialogue.

If you can make a man laugh, you can make him think.

—ALFRED EMANUEL SMITH

Humor is the lubricating oil of business. It prevents friction and wins goodwill.   —UNKNOWN

A sense of humor is part of the art of leadership, of getting along with people, of getting things done.
—DWIGHT D. EISENHOWER

It is often just as sacred to laugh as it is to pray.
—CHARLES R. SWINDOLL

PART THREE

YOUR SIGNATURE WORK . . .

like building your dream home

*J*ust as a house reflects the personality of those who live there, your work—whether it's a volunteer project, a part-time job, full-time parenting, or a career—reflects you. You decide the quality of the materials you use, the effort you put into the project, the pace at which you will build, the ways you will use your work to benefit others, and the satisfaction you gain from living there.

As the general contractor, you pour the foundation, put up the framework, add the walls and roof, do the electrical wiring, inset the doors and windows, and finish the inside of your house in stages.

You build your life's work in the same way—one day, one customer, one task, one project, or one goal at a time. Over a lifetime, you will have built a finished product—one that you can sign your name to with satisfaction.

> *Once a person says, "This is who I really am, what I am all about, what I was really meant to do," it is easier to decide how to spend one's time.* —DAVID VISCOTT

> *Get to know two things about a man—how he earns his money and how he spends it—and you have the clue to his character, for you have a searchlight that shows up the inmost recesses of the soul. You know all you need to know about his standards, his motives, his driving desires, his real religion.* —ROBERT J. McCRACKEN

FOURTEEN

READING THE BLUEPRINTS
Following a Plan to Arrive at the Payoff

If your life were a product or service, how much value would your designer label hold?

Do you see your work as a blessing or a curse?

Do you overwork? Are you defined by your work?

Is that a dead bug on the window, spoiling the view? I dashed downstairs for the window cleaner and a rag.

When we'd decided to build the two-story library years earlier, it sounded like a good idea. The architect recommended French doors that opened onto the balcony because we could look out over the entire lake from that vantage point. Never mind that the library "loft" is the size of a postage stamp and that the architect had created roof angles that made the water drain off in rivers around the front porch. But after five years of dealing with rainstorms and several leaks, we finally stumbled on a solution: install storm windows on the outside of the French doors so that all of them except one would be permanently closed.

Anxious to see how the solution worked, we had come home from the office and bolted up to the loft with high expectations of seeing the new view—only to have it marred by a smashed bug right at eye level.

Window spray to the rescue. I scrubbed the outside first. No luck. Strange. I was sure a dead bug wouldn't be on the *inside* of the house. But I marched inside, window cleaner in hand, to have a look.

A sinking feeling hit the pit of my stomach. *Five years for this?* Back onto the balcony for a second look. Sure enough, the bug had been smashed between the glass door and the new *permanently installed* storm window—suspended forever at eye level to mar an otherwise beautiful view of the lake from our library loft.

It seemed obvious to us that the installer would have noticed the bug when he started to nail the storm window to the door facing, but apparently caring enough about doing a good job to handle this "small" detail was not a part of his plan for the project. Technically, he'd installed the storm windows. I'm sure his contract didn't call for cleaning a bug off the windowpane.

A year later when we put the house up for sale, the "small" detail became an even bigger issue as potential buyers climbed to the loft to take a look at the view from the balcony. And every time we attend an "open house" for a friend or business colleague moving into a new home or office building, we think of that detail.

Traditionally, owners of brand-new homes throw a party, invite their friends and neighbors, and often include the professionals and craftspeople who have worked on the house—carpenters, bricklayers, roofers, the drapery maker, the cabinet maker, the architect, the interior decorator, the general contractor. They mingle with the other guests and friends, see how their work contributed to the finished product, and "take their bows" over a job well done. At those parties I often wonder if the installer of our storm windows would have been proud to show his son the loft window with encased bug. "This is the work your dad did today. This is my personal best."

And sometimes I wonder if CEOs, software analysts, and pharmaceutical salespeople can say the same thing to their children and friends at the end of a typical day: "This is the work I did today. I'm responsible here. This is my finest work—my personal best." If so, how so?

And if not—why not?

DO WE HAVE A PLAN?

"Are you enjoying your new job?" "How was your vacation—did you get lots of rest?" Sometimes people find it awkward to answer such questions because of a general confusion about the nature of work and play. Are we being punished or pampered from eight to five Monday through Friday?

Family vacations often bring this issue to a head. One spouse wants to arrive at the vacation destination and then find out what's available to do at the moment. If time works out and they have the proper gear and clothes with them, they do it. If timing, gear, or clothes don't work, no problem—they'll find something else equally enjoyable.

In contrast, the other spouse tackles the family vacation with the planning skills of an executive:

CARLA: I've got maps of the downtown area with the
      museums marked.

BRAD: How are we going to get there?

CARLA: Better to take the subway. There's no place to park
      down there. And it costs a small fortune. Besides that,
      we have to get back by three if we're going to make it
      to the El Frisborne by four. That's on highway 29, on the
      south side.

BRAD: And why are we going there? Maybe we should forget
      the matinee and take a nap.

CARLA: We don't have time for a nap.

BRAD: Are you sure the play's worth seeing?

CARLA: Yes, definitely. El Frisborne is one of the oldest theaters
      here, according to all the books that mentioned it. That's
      the only play we're going to have time to catch. I forgot to
      read the background on that—remind me to do that
      tonight when we get back to the hotel.

BRAD: Honey, you're going to be worn out. I thought you
      wanted to rest on this vacation.

CARLA: I *am* resting.

BRAD: No, you're not. You're planning, researching, rushing,
      reserving this, buying that, canceling the other. This
      vacation has been more work than . . . work.

CARLA: I don't know what you're talking about. It's a change
      of pace. I *love* it! This isn't work. It's fun!

Some of us have the same confusion about our jobs: Are we
supposed to love them or hate them? Is work work, or is work
fun? If it's supposed to be so enjoyable, why do we have TGIF
mugs and refer to Wednesdays as "hump" days and slap each

other on the back and comment, "You'll make it—you've got a long weekend coming up"?

Yet an equal number of those people who're supposed to be "playing" sneak back to "work." As Lisa Beamer recalled about her preschooler talking to his dad, Todd Beamer, a hero of United Flight 93, who was frequently caught "playing" (working?) with his technological gadgets on the weekend: "Pack it up, Dad." And he did. But not without a struggle—the struggle of finding time to do two things he loved—work, and play with his children.

In fact, look around you at an airport, a hotel, or a restaurant, and you'll see more and more people playing at work and working at play. Professionals pack their laptops along with their tennis rackets for family vacations. They check e-mail daily from their hotel rooms or send and receive text messages from their Palm Pilots during their stay at the dude ranch. They're accessible to clients or their bosses or colleagues 24/7. On the other hand, during their workday they're interacting with others, investigating creative design work, attending social functions to network for new clients, learning new skills, exploring new technological gadgets for far more hours than anyone expects—all because these activities are fun. Never mind that they're part of a "job."

Vernon and I have had the following conversation more than once. I spend many Sunday afternoons reading. He prefers to watch the football game or dig around in the flower garden. Suddenly, he'll dash in the house and say, "Wish you didn't have to stay inside and read. It's such a beautiful day outside."

"I know it is. I can see. But I'm enjoying myself reading."

"But that's working."

"No, it isn't."

"What are you reading?"

"*Publishers Weekly*. Newsletters. This new book."

"So it *is* work. I don't see how you can enjoy that." He shakes his head in disbelief.

"Well, maybe after a while I can find time to get in a little *fun* like you're having—hoeing a few weeds in one-hundred-degree heat until I get a few good blisters on my hands, a little dirt under my nails, and a backache."

"The garden really does need to be weeded. It will look a lot better."

He grins and saunters back outside. I sip another glass of iced tea with my feet propped up and then nap. He's playing, and I'm working. Or is it the other way around?

Even retirees vacillate between the two. Retirees leave their "play" and throng to "work" by the millions. Back to their old jobs on the same payroll or as "consultants" on a contract arrangement. Sometimes as CEOs in their own business. In a volunteer job for a nonprofit organization. For a community or political cause. As caretaker for their grandchildren. They go not necessarily for the money but for the pleasure of it.

And that view—whether you see your work as drudgery or fun—often determines how well you do it.

MONDAY-MORNING BLAHS OR BONANZA?

Is work a good thing or a bad thing? Your answer to this question will mark a major turning point in your life.

So let's get that matter decided: Is work a blessing or, well, a curse? a good thing or a bad thing? a means to an end or an "end"—meaningful and important to us—in and of itself?

B.C. Forbes, founder of *Forbes* magazine, answers like this: "Work is the meat of life; pleasure, the dessert."

The idea of work being a curse goes all the way back to the biblical account of creation and the Garden of Eden—when Adam and Eve were kicked out of the Garden for disobedience. But *having to work* wasn't their curse. They worked before the curse. God planted the Garden and told Adam to work and maintain it. God cursed the ground, not work. Adam's curse was having his work become *more difficult.* Eve's curse was having childbearing become painful.

Work, in and of itself, has never been part of the curse. How we do it can be difficult. It can be in a tough environment, with a jerk for a client or a boss. The marketplace can be dangerous, with dishonest dealings on every corner. The outcome can be disappointing. You may lose a sale to an unethical competitor, get laid off during a merger two months before retirement, or have a tornado destroy your building and demolish your product inventory, equipment, and client records.

But work itself has dignity; it is foundational to integrity. God himself was the first worker. He looked at his creation and said it was good.

And according to the the Bible there's profit in hard work: "All hard work brings a profit, but mere talk leads only to poverty" (Proverbs 14:23).

So how do we profit? What are the payoffs?

First, we make money. Obviously, these financial resources provide for ourselves and our family: "Make it your ambition to . . . work with your hands, just as we told you, so that your daily life may win the respect of outsiders and so that you will not be dependent on anybody" (1 Thessalonians 4:11-12). We can give away extra resources to support God's work in the world and other causes we believe in.

Working for this reason is a direct command from the Bible: "If anyone will not work, neither shall he eat" (2 Thessalonians 3:10, NKJV). The basic idea of our work is stewardship of God's creation—the resources he gives us as talents and skills and the circumstances he plunks us into as asset managers.

Second, work improves our emotional well-being. Solomon called finding satisfaction in one's work the gift of God (see Ecclesiastes 2:24; 3:12-13). Have you ever awakened in a gloomy mood and discovered that after you'd gone about your work, your outlook brightened somewhere during the day? Have you felt the stress and strain of a problem drain away as you did hard physical work or turned your attention to analyzing a work problem unrelated to the family problem that had you perplexed? After you directed your thinking away from your problems, nagging indecisiveness, or disappointments and toward your work, you gained renewed energy and came into contact with others who gave you good advice or encouragement.

Even those suffering from great loss—such as the death of a loved one or a debilitating disease—frequently find comfort in returning to their work (either a paid job or volunteer projects or at-home work) as soon as they can function physically. Having a routine that includes projects and interaction with others helps to heal the emotions.

Have you ever "lost yourself" in your work? Suds of satisfaction lather up unexpectedly from accomplishment. Work brings contentment.

Third, work "profits," or benefits, our character. Just as physical conditioning builds muscle, our will strengthens our endurance.

The sheer knowledge that we've "hung in there" and seen something difficult through to the end without quitting makes it easier the next time self-control becomes a test. What we go through in our work rubs the rough edges off our character— if we reflect on it and react to it appropriately. What we learn as we work shapes and sharpens responsibility, accountability, personality, and perspective.

So there you have it—three payoffs, or ways you profit, from your work: (1) you gain financial resources to support yourself, your family, and other causes, (2) you gain emotional well-being and contentment, and (3) you improve your character.

Are we saying that all work leads to financial gain? Absolutely *not*. Some people work hard all their lives and never earn more than they need to meet what most consider minimum requirements. In fact, my grandparents and great-grandparents worked extremely hard all their lives—as salt miners, store clerks, farmers, ranchers, homemakers—and no one would ever consider them wealthy.

You may choose to work without getting paid at all. You may work in the home. You may work as a volunteer in the community and in your church. I have a friend who has two master's degrees plus postgraduate work and has chosen to stay home ever since she married fifteen years ago and had two sons. There's no harder worker and stronger contributor in the school, church, and community than my friend Debbie. Work may have nothing to do with earning money. But work does lead to profit in other ways—ways related to enjoyment, relationships, dignity, character.

So if work is good, not bad, it stands to reason that you should give it your best shot.

Man must work. That is certain as the sun. But he may
work grudgingly or he may work gratefully; he may work
as a man or he may work as a machine. There is no work
so rude, that he may not exalt it; no work so impassive, that
he may not breathe a soul into it; no work so dull that he
may not enliven it.   —HENRY GILES

THE DESIGNER LABEL: YOU, INC.

Some people talk a good job—but fail to do it. Whoever first
made the observation "Big hat, no cattle" crammed a lot of truth
into four short words. In its origin, it meant that the cowboy
decked out in the finest western duds seldom owned the cattle
and big ranch he was bragging about.

It reminds me of the often reserved nature of the truly
wealthy. My dad has a friend in his midseventies who lives a
rather unassuming lifestyle and occasionally mentions driving
"up to the ranch" for an outing. Having grown up on a farm
himself, my dad never seemed too curious about this or that
trip until finally one day my dad asked his friend, "Carl, just
what size ranch do you have up there?"

"Oh, about forty-four thousand acres."

Some people *talk;* others *do.*

If you intend to *do* your personal best, what's the goal?

Second Corinthians 13:11 says, "Aim for perfection." Think
about it: An artist doesn't think while painting a landscape,
This tree looks a little out of proportion to the building beside it, but, oh
well, it's just a painting—not the real thing. Designer Georgio Armani
doesn't put his label on a suit that has the lining hanging out of
the jacket sleeve by an inch and say, "That'll work this month—
we'll just charge less for this one."

Imagine yourself working as You, Inc. That really is often the case in today's economy. Forty years ago the average worker had 1.5 jobs in a lifetime. Today, according to the U.S. Bureau of Labor Statistics report on workers born between 1957 and 1964, the typical worker in this age group held 9.6 jobs between the ages of 18 and 36. Companies no longer pay for someone to stay in a position; they pay for someone to produce results. If workers don't deliver outcomes, companies replace them. Likewise, employees look to employers to provide challenging experiences, meaningful work, training, advancement, and opportunities to grow. When that's not the case, they may move on to other organizations.

So consider yourself as the builder and owner of You, Inc. You have value to contribute. You're opening up shop every day from eight to five. As the builder, you're signing the projects you created for the day. What value does your personal label hold? What perception does it create in the minds of your coworkers, supervisors, or clients? Consider the pride with which some people wear an Armani suit or a Rolex watch or decorate with designer sheets. Labels signify a certain level of quality. Do others feel as special to be assigned to your projects, your team, or your department?

Artists frequently say they have to "get in the mood" to create. Actors aim to "get inside the mind" of the characters they portray and ask directors about what their "motivation" is as they play the scene. A novelist setting a mystery in Scotland travels there to absorb the culture, see the streets, eat in the restaurants, and visit the shops. Olympic athletes motivate themselves with a mental rehearsal as they get alone and focus on the goal—the big win.

So in the same vein as these other professionals, consider your own "mental preparation" and motivation—in builders' vocabulary, the blueprint—for your work. You want what you're building to meet exacting standards: You want the finished product to reflect as much attention to the small details as to the overall design. In other words, your blueprint doesn't include a squashed bug between two panes of glass. The biblical standard is nothing short of excellence: "Whatever your hand finds to do, do it with all your might" (Ecclesiastes 9:10). It's not about being satisfied with doing the minimum. It's about striving for the best possible finished product.

Michelangelo was known for the long hours he worked. An acquaintance once asked him about his work on the cathedral dome, "Why be so careful with every little detail? No one can see it from down here." He answered, "God sees it, and when you work for God, you work well."

When your goal is to do your work with excellence because you see that as a direct command of God, that's all the motivation you need. And you don't have to worry about success or failure: "Commit to the Lord whatever you do, and your plans will succeed," says Proverbs 16:3. That success may come in the form of peace of mind, control, admiration, self-respect, influence with others, money, fame, or heavenly reward. But that success—in whatever form God chooses to give it—comes directly from him.

WHAT DOES EXCELLENCE LOOK LIKE?

Let's get specific. Whether you are an accountant, lawyer, engineer, service agent, full-time mother, administrative assistant, teacher, minister, homemaker, or software programmer, what exactly would excellence look like in your work arena? In my twenty-four years as consultant to some of the largest corporations in the country, I've gathered quite a bit of data on what makes someone a peak performer. The list below may tickle your thinking until you can narrow it down more specifically to the work you did, say, last Tuesday afternoon:

- You schedule the work appropriately.
- You decide how and when to use emotional energy.
- You cultivate broad interests so that you're always learning and growing.
- You keep commitments.
- You meet deadlines.
- You act instead of watching others act.
- You take initiative.
- You demonstrate a positive attitude of service.
- You accept responsibility for results, not just for activity.
- You are accountable for making improvements and contributing ideas.
- You show a return on the investment of assets and resources entrusted to your use.

On the other hand, sometimes it helps to understand what something is by focusing on what it is not. In those same twenty-four years I've also gathered plenty of data about what makes someone's work a dismal disappointment. As a contrast to the list of practices leading to excellence in your work, here's a short list that almost guarantees work failure:

- You do no more than what's required.
- You leave things until the last minute before the deadline so that you are working under maximum internal and external pressure.

- You never double-check your work, assuming that someone else will catch any errors.
- You get angry and defensive if anyone questions you.
- You point out others' mistakes if they discover yours.
- You blame circumstances or other people when results turn out less desirable than expected.
- You pout, never analyze what went wrong, and refuse to learn anything for the future.

> *The difference between failure and success is doing a thing nearly right and doing it exactly right.*
>
> —EDWARD C. SIMMONS

Aristotle observed that "we are what we repeatedly do. Excellence, then, is not an act, but a habit." Excellence is not something we slip into and out of. We don't perform well one day but not the next. According to Aristotle, we don't work with excellence because we are good; we do excellent work because we are in the habit of doing all things with excellence.

In short, excellence grows on you. Just as you can trace an artist's growth toward maturity through the years, so our work, what we are "building," should become more excellent. Each project that we "sign" should be our personal best at the moment.

The young son of nineteenth-century publisher Elbert Hubbard thought he'd pinpointed such a man when he suggested that Andrew Summers Rowan might actually be the biggest hero of the Spanish-American War. Rowan received the Distinguished Service Cross for his effort. Although he served in several other posts after his most famous mission and lived until 1943, Rowan's greatest contribution to our country was the inspiration that he unknowingly provided as the central character in Hubbard's *A Message to Garcia*.

Elbert Hubbard penned his masterpiece one evening in an hour, after a trying day at the office. As the family talked about the day over dinner, Hubbard's son Bert pointed out that it was like Rowan, the man who could "carry the message to Garcia":

When war broke out between Spain and the United States, it was essential that America be able to communicate quickly with Garcia, the leader of the insurgents. Garcia was somewhere in the mountains in Cuba—no one knew where—and no mail or telegraph could reach him. Someone told the president that if anybody could find Garcia and get a message to him, a guy by the name of Rowan could.

They sent for Rowan, gave him a letter, and told him to deliver it.

Garcia stalked into the vast Cuban jungle and three weeks later came out on the other side, having delivered the letter.

The analogy hit Elbert Hubbard like a flash. He went on to make this point: He did not intend to tell *how* Rowan accomplished this feat. His point was that Rowan *did* it. He accomplished his mission with excellence. The remainder of Hubbard's tale talks about how wonderful it would be to have dependable, competent people who do excellent work—people you can depend on no matter what.

But the real story behind the story is what happened after its publication. It struck such a chord with people—business owners and managers, military leaders, government officials—that requests for reprints began to pour in from around the world, including Russia, Germany, France, Spain, Japan, and China. With more than 100 million copies in print,

A Message to Garcia is listed as the fifth best-seller of all time, according to the *Book of Lists*.

To paraphrase Elbert Hubbard, were he alive today and shopping at Wal-Mart: In every organization on the planet today, there's a search for just such a person. People like this can almost name their salary and their working conditions. Any president, director, spouse, colleague, client, or friend would give almost anything to have such a person at their side— a person who can "carry a message to Garcia."

When your work speaks for itself, don't interrupt.

—HENRY J. KAISER

IS WORK A TRIVIAL PURSUIT OR A DEFINING STATEMENT?

So when does the pursuit of excellence turn into overwork? If work is good, isn't more work better? Not necessarily. It depends on the motivation and the results.

First, let's look at motivation: There seem to be two extreme views about work: (1) You *are* your work, and (2) your work is just what you have to do to get what you want. Both extremes will lead you astray in how you work.

People who think they *are* their work tend to overwork. People who think work is just a way to get what they want tend to treat it as a "necessary evil" of life and give it less than their best—often much less. This second extreme will be a topic of the next few chapters, so we'll put that aside until later.

People who overwork may have many emotions and needs warring inside: Fear of not being able to provide for the family. Fear that God can't or won't take care of their needs. Anxiety about competition from others. A need to feel needed and significant. A need to belong to a work group as a substitute for "family." A drive to feel important and to be recognized for achievements. A need to be in control. A desire for material possessions.

Overwork for these reasons falls short of the mark of excellence and leads to inordinate emotional and physical weariness. The only way out of such a predicament is to remember the One you're working for—God—who promises, "Come to me, all you who are weary and burdened, and I will give you rest" (Matthew 11:28).

Remember, too, that all overwork doesn't happen on the job. It can happen at home or at church. We used to have a neighbor who worked at home rather than outside at a paying job. But as a stay-at-home mom with three small children, she did not—stay at home, that is. Walk into her house on any given day, and she had a myriad of projects going: sewing, baking, acting as director of a community theater production, selling lingerie through a catalog company, volunteering as a teacher's aide at the school, working on church committees, helping out at her husband's office when someone didn't show up. She frequently broke into tears from sheer exhaustion.

Overwork happens at many churches. Often, regular attenders are so busy on the weekends, running from activity to activity and meeting to meeting, that they head back to their jobs on Monday morning too exhausted to do their regular work. Their churches have failed to model what the Bible says about taking a day of rest.

Where's the balance? What are the guidelines? Rest rejuvenates our spirits and restores us to the habit of excellence in our work. Rest is biblical.

But although the idea of rest is biblical, the idea of retirement as our culture defines it—spending one's days engaged only in "play" and leisure activities—is not. At some point, your paying job may end. You may decide that you have enough money and want to stop being paid for your efforts. But nowhere does God say that it's good for us to pack in our gear, our skills, and our knowledge and take a long hike out to the wilderness of forever.

Your doctor won't tell you that either. He or she will tell you that work of some kind will keep your mind more alert and your body healthier than inactivity and leisure.

So to do your personal best, find your balance. Work is not a trivial pursuit, an incidental way to make ends meet and pay for what you want or spend your time between the weekends. But neither does it define your reason for existence.

> *It is our best work that God wants, not the dregs of our exhaustion. I think he must prefer quality to quantity.*
> —GEORGE MACDONALD

Adding the Finishing Touches to Your Dream Home

Even in building their dream home, people have moments of doubt about whether the process is a pain or a joy, whether the effort will lead to trivial pursuits or add meaning to their life.

Work crews don't always show up when expected. Materials sometimes arrive damaged. Accidents may occur that result in delay after delay.

The same thing happens in our work. We find ourselves continually going back to our plans and reevaluating them and the payoff for our efforts. As you build your dream career or do volunteer work, understand that the process can be wearing at times, but the payoff is powerful if you keep your work in perspective. Don't let your work *define* you; instead, let it *refine* you. Take ownership of it. Be accountable for it. Sign it with excellence.

> *Integrate what you believe into every single area of your life. Take your heart to work and ask the most and best of everybody else.* —MERYL STREEP

> *The secret of joy in work is contained in one word— excellence. To know how to do something well is to enjoy it.* —PEARL S. BUCK

> *The man who does not work for the love of work but only for money is not likely to make money nor to find much fun in life.* —CHARLES M. SCHWAB

FIFTEEN

LAYING THE FOUNDATION

Discovering Your Calling and Equipment

*H*ow do you know you've found your calling?

*W*hat "power tools" have you been given?

AT ALMOST every decade in their lives, people seem to struggle with the need to find or reaffirm their calling, their purpose in life. With so much focus on the spiritual in today's workplace, we often hear people talk about their work as their calling, or vocation. They understand and experience the fulfillment of a big part of their calling or purpose in life through their work.

College students fret that changing majors may cause them to "lose hours" or lock them into a career they'll regret for decades. Twenty-somethings talk to recruiters about their plans and life's purpose and panic when they realize that accepting one job offer shuts down other offers and avenues—maybe forever. Thirty-somethings reflect on their life's purpose again, wondering how much risk they can afford to take in making a career change when realities don't match their expectations about salary, promotions, or the thrill of the deal.

Parents may reexamine their calling when their kids move out. They wonder what higher purpose could possibly occupy their time for the next several decades. People in midlife wake up one month bored and ask themselves, *Do I really want to keep doing this the rest of my life? Should I change tracks before it's too late— it's now or never.* People late in their careers or at retirement age look back and wonder, *Have I done anything that really matters? Have I made a mark?*

People facing various crises such as the loss of a job, a divorce, a serious illness, or the death of a loved one ask, "Was my work 'beside the point'? Did I lose my balance? Have I been confused all along about what's really important in life? Have I lost my way?"

All of these are crossroads of calling. And developing a sense of calling or purpose implies believing in a God who calls us.

> *A man without purpose is like a ship without a rudder.*
> —THOMAS CARLYLE

Am I called to my work? It's a good question to ask. Finding meaning in what we do motivates us. Serving other people through our work produces a profound sense of significance and satisfaction.

So to build our "work" house to fit our lifestyle, we need to have a photo of what it should look like. Most homeowners visit model homes and homes of their friends, devour magazines and search Web sites, and talk with consultants, designers, and architects before they select a site and narrow their choices to the few specialists they'll trust with building their dream home.

Because God is the One who calls us, it only makes sense that we'd make sure our photo matches his photo—that our plans and purpose match his plans and purpose for us: " 'I know the plans I have for you,' declares the Lord, 'plans to prosper you, . . . to give you hope and a future' " (Jeremiah 29:11).

You may frequently hear people say, "I'm no good at accounting. I just hate crunching numbers all day. That's just not my *"calling."* Or, "He was *called* into the ministry when he was seventeen at a youth camp." Or, "I felt *called* to go to New York to work with the victims of the terrorist attacks and do what I could to help for a couple of weeks." Or, "I love working with children. They're so eager to learn, so much more receptive than adults. Working with children from disadvantaged homes in this city-wide program—that's my *calling.*"

While each of these expressions about *calling* is different, the concept of calling encompasses all of them. God calls us to be his children and to participate in his greater plan for the universe in whatever form those activities may take. And that calling for us may or may not involve a specific job or work assignment. Our calling involves our whole life—not just the hours from nine to five. In fact, to think of calling as something that involves only those who go into "full-time" ministry misses the whole idea. That said, most of us do discover that our calling is connected to our work throughout our lifetime.

CALLING CANNOT BE OVERSOLD

Every corporation on the planet would do well to help people find their calling for two significant reasons:

- Having every worker doing what he or she does best would increase corporate profits dramatically.
- All workers would feel passionate about their work.

Both individuals and the organizations they work for benefit from having an understanding of the idea of calling. As John Naisbitt and Patricia Aburdene pointed out in *Re-Inventing the Corporation* (Warner Books, 1985) almost two decades ago, when you identify with a company's purpose and experience ownership in a shared vision, you find yourself "doing your life's work instead of just doing time."

The difference in your emotional investment in a "job" versus a "calling" is much like the difference in the financial investment you're willing to make in a rental property versus a house you're personally going to live in. For example, let's say you earn a hefty bonus for a brilliant idea or you inherit a large sum of money. Let's consider a couple ways you could spend that money.

Scenario 1: You already have a nice place to live and all of your needs are met, so you decide to use the inheritance money to invest in real estate. You purchase property that will generate rental income. Now, how much time do you spend selecting the carpet and paint color? How much time selecting the flooring? How much time selecting window treatments?

Scenario 2: Let's say you don't have a nice place to live yourself, so you decide to take the bonus or inheritance money and put it toward building your own house. How much time and energy do you spend selecting the carpet and paint color? How much time selecting flooring? How much time selecting the exterior brick color?

Your "mission" in scenario 2 makes a great deal of difference in your financial investment, doesn't it? The same is true of your emotional investment—or lack thereof—when you feel that your work is—or isn't—your calling. Your level of investment will either pay off or plummet in value.

If you don't think calling comes high on the priority list, consider these examples of complaints from square pegs trying to fit into round holes in the workplace:

- "I'm bored out of my mind. Same ole, same ole. Day after day. Month after month. Year after year. And for what? A lousy paycheck."

- "Maybe I'm in over my head. I want to do a good job— I really do. But my boss is just never pleased. I've been passed over for promotions several times. I'm treading water, and I know it. It's the best I can do, and it's not good enough."

- "When I walk out of here on the weekends, I feel like a heavy weight has been lifted off my shoulders. And on Sunday night when I start thinking about facing Monday morning, I get a knot in the pit of my stomach."

- "I hate all this travel. It's killing my marriage. And I don't even know my kids anymore. But if you're going to do what I do, you have to travel—that's what this career's all about."

- "I do okay. Make a lot of money. But somehow the old excitement just isn't there anymore."

- "They've got me in golden handcuffs. My retirement plan and benefits are superb. I'd never find that anywhere else. Just another ten years, and I can retire and do something I really enjoy."

It sounds as if these people are serving a sentence, not fulfilling a calling. Whether they know it or not, they may have missed their calling—and consequently the deep satisfaction that goes along with it.

> *When work is a pleasure, life is a joy. When work is duty,*
> *life is slavery.*
> —MAKSIM GORKY

HOW DO YOU IDENTIFY YOUR CALLING?

Although we've just defined calling as much broader than your work life, for our purposes here, we're going to be talking about calling as it relates to your work—whether at a paid job or career, a volunteer job or project, or at-home work.

Generally, there are three *P*s that will help you identify your vocational calling and help you build Your Signature Work: power tools and provisions; passion, and plot, or path. If you're counting, you'll realize that there are really five words beginning with *P*, but because some of them are closely connected, we'll treat them as three elements.

Power Tools and Provisions

Power tools and *provisions* are those things you've been given to work with—the hammers, saws, nails, drills, ladders, paint buckets you use—as you "build" Your Signature Work. More specifically, though, power tools and provisions are the skills, talents, aptitudes, personality traits, and spiritual gifts that you use to accomplish whatever work assignments come your way. These are the tools and provisions God has given you to enable you to make your way in the world and to fulfill his calling and purpose for you.

Passion

Your natural interests, creative urges, and the sheer joy you experience when doing certain things also provide a clue to your calling. Originally, an amateur was someone who did something strictly for the love of doing it—not for pay as a professional. Through the years, though, the word has taken on a negative connotation, so that now it often means someone who is "less skilled" than a professional who receives money for services. But for our discussion here in finding your calling, consider what you *love* to do—what you would do even if no one paid you for doing it. Often, these are the projects that you take on in your "spare" time simply because they interest you. They make your creative juices flow; they make you lose all track of time when you're doing them; and they give you great satisfaction. When you talk about them, your face lights up, and your voice and body become animated. In a word, you're *passionate* about that kind of work.

Plot or Path

A plot is an opportunity or an option—that is, a plot of ground or something to build on. A path leads to that plot, or opportunity. For example, you may feel *passionate* about traveling and living abroad, and you have an unusual aptitude *(power tool)* for learning languages and speak four languages fluently. Now, someone offers you a job as a foreign-language interpreter in Peru. That's a clear plot of ground upon which to build Your Signature Work. All you need to do is follow where the path takes you. If that job ends, you follow the path to the next plot of opportunity and continue building. If you're finding no plot of opportunity or path leading you there, you can be sure your calling is something or somewhere else.

I never feel age. . . . If you have creative work, you don't
have age or time.   —LOUISE NEVELSON

I feel just such a passion for what I do. I lose all sense of time and place, completely losing myself in creating words on paper. From about the age of twelve until sixteen, I felt God tugging my heart in that direction, but it took me four years to tell anyone about my internal struggle because I couldn't put language around that sense of calling. So at the age of sixteen when I shared with my church my commitment to God's plan, the response was, "Are you going to be a preacher's wife or a missionary?" Timidly I answered first one and then another well-meaning church member, "Maybe so. I don't know who I'm going to marry. And I have no inclination to be a missionary."

It was not until I was twenty-seven and had two young children and a husband who was struggling with mental illness that I understood how to connect my God-given passion and my set of skills. After teaching school for one year, I had no desire to repeat the same process with a new set of students. In a counseling session with an educational director at my church, I expressed my lack of enthusiasm for teaching, and in return the counselor probed, "So what do you really like to do?"

"Well, I don't know what I could do to earn a living."

"No, no," he pushed. "I didn't ask you what you could do to make a living. I asked you what you *liked* to do—what you're *good* at doing."

"Well, I've never thought about a job in that way. But I like

to write. Or I used to. I always loved writing English composi-
tions in high school and college. I made good grades. English
lit was my major. But how could I ever make a living writing?"

"I don't know," he said. "But I'd suggest you find out."

That afternoon I drove to the public library and checked
out every book I could find on careers involving writing—from
producing greeting-card verses to romance novels to inspira-
tional how-tos.

I tossed and turned for three sleepless nights as I worried
about what my future would hold. I turned over in my mind
the offer I'd had to write a series of Bible study materials for
my denomination and reexamined the sense of calling I had as
a teenager.

At three o'clock in the morning I pulled on my robe and
padded into the family room with my Bible. "God, I don't know
what you have for me to do with my life, or how I'm going to
support this family. I want with all my heart to become a writer,
but I don't see how I can make a living at it. Lord, you've just
got to give me an answer—now. I need sleep." A sense of peace
I'd never experienced before fell over me. "Write." I said it aloud,
closed my Bible, and headed down the hallway back to bed.
And to sleep.

The following morning I offered my resignation as a teacher,
effective three weeks later at midterm. My principal told me
it "just so happened" there was a school board meeting that
evening. "If you want to resign, they'll certainly honor your
decision. The school board vote is merely a formality in such
matters."

Driving to school the next morning, I heard the local school
board meeting news on the radio. "The school board met in

regular session last night. . . ." The monotone droned on until this line caught my attention. "The board voted *not* to accept Dianna Booher's resignation, citing the fact that the district had no other applicants qualified to teach Spanish." *Not* to accept? Had I heard it correctly?

So much for clarity of calling. I spent the next four long days perplexed. On the fifth day I received a note to report to the principal's office during my conference period. "I just got a call from a woman who's moving back here to take care of her mother, who is ill," the principal explained. "And she's looking for a teaching job at midterm or sooner. Spanish."

My calling seemed clear after all.

Now, after writing forty-one books and founding a corporate communication training company, I can affirm that when God places a passion in your heart, he has a plan and a purpose. It only stands to reason then, that if you have the three *P*s—the power tools and provisions, the passion, and the plot or path— that you'll find the right job, the one that matches the way God designed you, and the job that requires someone with just your abilities, passion, and personality.

TESTING THE FIRMNESS OF THE FOUNDATION

We're a nation of Monday-morning quarterbacks. We second-guess our presidents, our war heroes, our CEOs, our favorite new college grads on every decision they make. So it's not surprising that we'd do the same thing to ourselves when it comes to our own career choices. We look for affirmation that we've found our calling since our sense of calling is the foundation on which we build our Signature Work.

Once again, three *P*s may help in our evaluation:

Praise

Do others recognize the skills, talents, personality traits, or spiritual gifts in you and comment on them? Of course, your motivation or intention as you work is not to receive praise from others for what you do. But typically that's the form their comments take when they see you exercise your "power tools" in living out your calling: "The way you take all this data and analyze the problem so quickly amazes me." Or, "You always seem to help the team come to a decision—you always get the team focused without making them angry." Or, "You really have a knack for decorating without spending a lot of money." Or, "Everything you touch seems to turn to gold. Your advice on our investments has really been invaluable in allowing our nonprofit organization to fund the projects we needed to handle this year." Such comments affirm to you that others recognize your power tools when they see them in use.

Positive Results

How do things turn out when you use your power tools (skills, talents, personality, spiritual gifts) with passion, on this plot of opportunity? What are the results of your work? Are they positive or negative? If things typically turn out well in your work, that's a clear sign that you're living out your calling. If they don't, that's cause for question. At this point you may be thinking, *I know people who are just plain good at everything and excel at whatever they do. Their results are always good, and they always receive praise. How can those people be sure they're following their true calling?* Just as the first set of three *P*s are connected and work together in helping you identify your calling, these three *P*s don't function in isolation either. So even if praise and positive results are often present, you'll also need to take into account the following third *P*.

Peace

If you're working at a job or on a specific assignment that God has called you to, you'll feel a growing sense of peace that you're "in the right place at the right time." Peace, rather than panic, will rule in your heart of hearts. You'll feel settled rather than restless and have a clear sense that this is "it" for the time being.

Just as the foundation of a building must be solid if the building is to be able to withstand the wearing elements of time, weather, temperature, and so forth, the foundation of your calling has to be solid in order for you to experience satisfaction as you face job changes, work on committee projects, or donate time to charities.

So to recap, identify your calling in light of the first three *P*s:

- *P*ower tools and *P*rovisions (skills, talents, personality traits, spiritual gifts)
- *P*assion
- *P*lot of opportunity or *P*ath leading to it

Then consider the additional three *P*s to reaffirm your sense of that calling:

- *P*raise from others when they recognize that you're exercising your gifts
- *P*ositive results
- *P*eace

These *P*s will provide assurance that you are doing work that's connected to your calling—whether your specific assignment is developing creative solutions, delivering carpet, or discounting crabmeat.

> *What I wanted was to be allowed to do the thing in the world that I did best—which I believed then and believe now is the greatest privilege there is. When I did that, success found me.* —DEBBI FIELDS

BEING COMMITTED TO YOUR CALLING

Where calling is concerned, two key principles matter a great deal: *commitment* and *gratitude*.

Commitment

The first key principle of calling is *commitment*. You have to be committed to finding out what your calling is. You can't count on someone's sending you an overnight package with a note inside: "Your mission, should you decide to accept it, is to do X."

On first blush you might think that's not such a bad idea after all. But let's go back to our house-building metaphor. You may be familiar with the organization called Habitat for Humanity, a nonprofit group that helps people in need to build a house through the use of donated materials and volunteer labor. But Habitat for Humanity is not a giveaway program. Homeowners must not only make a down payment and monthly mortgage payments; they must also agree to contribute a certain number of hours to the work effort ("sweat equity") unless health problems prevent them from doing so. This work requirement establishes accountability and builds pride in ownership.

The same is true about your calling as it relates to your work. To commit to discovering your calling proves part of the accountability of living out your calling. Your passion and peace grow in the pursuit of discovery and affirmation.

Gratitude

The second key principle of calling is *gratitude*. Be grateful for God's gifts of your "power tools," your natural passion, and your plot of opportunities. When any one of the three disappears, some of the joy of living out your calling fades. When your skill or talent grows rusty, you'll feel a sense of disappointment. Failing health—particularly mental health—can dim your natural interest or passion about your calling. Never take your calling for granted. Be grateful for the richness it adds to your life.

FINDING CRACKS IN THE FOUNDATION

What is true of any great blessing is also true of your work: Cracks in the foundation of your calling may cause Your Signature Work to weaken or even to fall into shambles.

A primary crack in the foundation forms when we start comparing our gifts, skills, talents, or opportunities to those of our friends and colleagues. Envy and jealousy may set in. The Parable of the Talents in the Gospel of Matthew clearly explains this truth: God gives different talents and opportunities to different people, and he expects different results from each according to what talents they've received. He rewards people according to how they perform with what they've been given.

In short, God doesn't "grade on a curve." Let's say Bradley makes twenty million dollars before he's thirty years old and gives five million dollars to starving children in Bangladesh.

Then he becomes a brain surgeon and saves the lives of 2,339 people before becoming an evangelist who preaches to millions around the world and builds six hospitals and fourteen schools.

Now let's say Gary drives a truck for thirty-five years. He serves his customers well, as if serving God himself, and influences everyone he comes in contact with because of his strong faith in God, his character, and right living—all of which lead seventeen family members and friends to put their faith in God.

If both men are equally living out their calling, God is equally pleased. There is no need for Gary to compare his gifts and opportunities to Bradley's and feel that his have less significance.

A second crack in the foundation of calling would be for Bradley to become prideful of his own gifts and opportunities. It happens. A minister may think his service to God is greater than that of his church members. A senator may think her service to God is greater than that of her constituents. Business owners may think their calling is greater than that of their workers.

A third crack may form when people forget stewardship altogether. That is, they bury their gifts, talents, or opportunities and don't use them at all or use them only for themselves. Philippians 2:4 reminds us: "Each of you should look not only to your own interests, but also to the interests of others." God does not give us our callings and gifts to use only on ourselves and our interests. He wants us to invest them in serving others.

I do not want to die until I have faithfully made the most of my talent and cultivated the seed that was placed in me until the last small twig has grown. —KATHE KOLLWITZ

So, to keep your foundation strong, don't compare your calling, talents, or gifts with those of others. Be humble. Use your calling in the service of others. These principles will keep cracks from forming in your foundation.

Adding the Finishing Touches to Your Dream Home

Have you ever walked into the home of someone you've never met—maybe as a guest at a party, as a friend of a friend, or as a stranger helping out in an emergency? You can learn much about the homeowners simply through observation. The refrigerator and cupboards or pantry will tell you what foods they enjoy and probably how often or how seldom they eat at home. An entertainment center or shelves will provide clues about their tastes in books and music. Trophies, equipment, or photos give hints about favorite sports. You might be able to guess their favorite colors. If you're there for very long, you'll notice which rooms they use often and which they seldom enter. The longer they've lived there, typically, the closer the house fits their personality and lifestyle.

That's as it should be. In fact, when people are in the market for a new home, they frequently walk into a house, look around, and say to the real estate agent, "This just isn't me."

Yet those same people may go to work every day to a job that just isn't "them." It's no wonder they feel frustrated, bored, burned out. If you need a house that fits your lifestyle—a temporary shelter that can be moved into or out of, traded up or down, remodeled or repaired—think how much more crucial it is to have work that matches who you are and your life's mission.

If you routinely feel like a square peg in a round hole, commit to discovering your calling. With a sense of calling, you can experience layoffs, job changes, relationship losses, and other tragedies and still know that you're exactly where you should be. And that's a really peaceful place to live.

> *To be successful, the first thing to do is fall in love with your work.* —SISTER MARY LAURETTA

> *The force, the mass of character, mind, heart or soul that a man can put into any work, is the most important factor in that work.* —A. P. PEABODY

SIXTEEN

FASHIONING THE FRAMEWORK
Building Meaning into the Mundane

*H*ow can you motivate yourself to push paper or answer the phone all day?

*W*ill what you do today matter a hundred years from now? Should you care?

*W*ho has more value in God's eyes—a minister, a movie mogul, or a maintenance manager?

AS SOMEONE has observed about beauty, what is mundane is also "in the eye of the beholder."

Just how excited do you think an airport rental-car agent can be about having to ask hundreds of times a week, "Would you like a Toyota Corolla or a Ford Taurus?" "Do you want to purchase a tank of gasoline, or do you plan to fill it up before you return the car?" "Will you be taking the insurance coverage, or will you be responsible for any damages to the car?"

On the other hand, you might link up with a rental agent who has a different take altogether on the job. Here's what one agent has to say about her service: "I consider it a real challenge to keep myself fresh with the routine, to keep from sounding like I've asked those questions a hundred times before. Customers drag themselves up to the counter, and they're tired, stressed out. Missed flights all day. Still another hour or two to drive until they get to their hotel for the night. What they don't need is another hassle. I take it as my personal goal to refresh them. Make them smile. Show them a little concern. Help them find their way to their destination a little quicker. Upgrade them when I can. The little things. You can just see the strain in their faces melt away. They walk away a little less stressed, with a little more energy for the last hour or two of their trip. It makes a real difference to them."

Ask a manager what she considers her major work, and she might say, "Recruiting new people and developing their strengths, leading my team to complete their projects on time within budget, and thinking about new ways to cut costs and improve efficiency."

The CEO of the same company might respond that mundane work is, "Recruiting new people and thinking about ways to cut costs and improve efficiency." He considers his major, challenging work to be latching on to a new product idea or developing an innovative plan for penetrating a new market.

Ask one mother what she considers her life's work, and she may complain that her time and talents are wasted, that all she does is wipe runny noses, do laundry, drive carpools, referee squabbles, and run to the dry cleaners. But a mother down the street may grow excited about staying home all day and doing the most important work she'll ever do—educating her children, tempering their dispositions, and molding their character.

The point is that what people consider "mundane" varies. And that's good news. God doesn't have a hierarchy of jobs or careers, with some more worthy than others. In our culture, of course, we frequently do. We have our lists of the Ten Best Dressed Women of the Year, the Fifty Richest People in America, the Five Hundred Fastest Growing Companies in the Country.

If you were to ask a thousand people in our culture to arrange occupations into a hierarchical list based on status in society, most would come up with something that looks like what we see on the left side of the following chart. Then if you asked them the reasons for their choices, you'd hear something similar to the comments in the column on the right.

Cultural Perception	Cultural Reasoning
Missionaries, ministers, priests	They do "spiritual" work.
Professional athletes, movie stars	They make lots of money. They're famous. Others serve them.
Doctors, teachers, counselors, social workers, parents, charity fund-raisers	They help other people live better lives—physically, spiritually, emotionally, mentally.
Judges, Supreme Court justices	They have power and respect.
CEOs, executives, business owners	They work with their "brains," have power and exercise control, and make money.
Software designers, lawyers	They work with their "brains" and have the potential to make a lot of money and become famous.
Stockbrokers, salespeople	They work with their "brains" and have the potential to make a lot of money but rarely become famous.
Police officers, firefighters	They help other people, but they work primarily with their hands, so they don't make much money. They don't become famous.
Roofers, truck drivers, store clerks, community volunteers	They work primarily with their hands. They don't make much money. They sometimes donate their services.

Fortunately, God doesn't have such a shallow ranking system. Power, money, control, and fame don't enter the picture. The following chart shows how God might shuffle the various work roles and his reasons for doing so.

God's View of Work	God's Report Card for Current Year
Bill Williams (plumber), Sid Cassady (parent), Vladimir Novokov (cancer researcher), Deborah Notonok (charity fund-raiser), Juan Salinas (church pianist)	Diligent, faithful, honest under stress, serves others, follows through on commitments, acts courageously against strong-but-wrong popular opinion
Philip Heist (dentist), Sheri Slusher (administrative assistant), Andy Smith (janitor), Babs Graham (school board member)	Serves fellow workers, customers, and community; demonstrates loyalty; shares faith in the marketplace
Maria Gonzales (pet store owner), Nadia Limosnero (pediatrician), Fred Snale (coach), Lou Gray (graphic artist), Tseuko Wai (pharmacist)	Provides for family, meets others' needs, demonstrates leadership on moral issues, honors commitments
Tyler Jones (farmer), Kevin Hart (politician), Mike LeRoy (sociologist), Barry Hickman (nurse)	Working on building personal character, being compassionate, doing quality work to serve others
Sandra McVeigh (accountant), Noel Court (bricklayer), Eric White (salesperson)	Sees work as a vehicle for offering praise, demonstrates honesty when dealing with tough situations
Donna Duncan (soloist), Tammy Taylor (hairdresser), Barb Bratcher (teacher), Mark Hartman (CEO)	Disappointing: wastes talents and skills, nonproductive, can't get along with coworkers
Roy Epps (minister), Robert Gray (surgeon), M. T. Boles (taxi driver), Susan Fitz (dietitian), Matt Tulloh (mayor)	Failure: Has bad attitude, prideful, hates serving others, greedy

From the simplest to the most magnificent buildings, all have nails, load-bearing beams, window latches, and floor tacks. They all began with a foundation and then had the walls framed in. Though the framed walls or window latches or floor tacks may never be showcased in *Better Homes and Gardens,* may not be available in the season's latest colors, and may even end up hidden from view, they can be vital to the safety of a building or necessary to efficient operation. Even these seemingly uninteresting parts of construction work must be done well because they contribute to the quality of the finished product.

The same is true of some work assignments. They may not land us on Wall Street, in the movies, or among the cultural elite, but they may be vitally important to our Signature Work and to God's kingdom.

> *It is not where you serve, but how you serve.*
>
> —J. RUBIN CLARK

IT'S NOT WHAT YOU DO, BUT WHY YOU DO IT

I've had a myriad of jobs since my teenage years: department store clerk, part-time secretary, tutor, kindergarten teacher, freelance journalist, seamstress, baby-sitter, data-entry clerk, file clerk, administrative assistant, Spanish teacher, English teacher, corporate trainer, consultant, CEO, author, software developer, speaker. As a department store clerk at age eighteen, I was allowed to make some major judgment calls regarding customer issues. And as a CEO and speaker traveling around the world, I've made copies and done filing. The point is that our focus should not be on the status of a task but on the quality of the work we do, not on the who but the how—not the task itself but on its purpose.

> *It is not what a man does that determines whether his work is sacred or secular, it is why he does it.* —A. W. TOZER

In every endeavor of life—sports, hobbies, play as well as work—motivation comes from the heart. Have you ever watched a store employee walk so slowly you thought she might fall over at any moment? Have you ever waited on a low-energy person to sack your groceries? Have you ever held the telephone receiver while someone double-checked your records and it seemed as if he'd gone to lunch and left you on hold? If so, then you understand the concept of a halfhearted effort.

Don't let the "mundane" mind-set or label lull you into thinking that what you do and how well you do it doesn't really matter. We've mentioned the fact that what people view as mundane varies from person to person and from job to job. A vice president might consider interviewing applicants for a new managerial position a "mundane" task; an engineer might love to have the authority to do so. An artisan might consider retiling a floor a "mundane" job but trimming a shower with accent pieces an art form.

Whatever you think of as mundane, consider that job for a moment. Doing what we consider mundane develops several aspects of our character: humility, discipline, perseverance, loyalty, gratitude, and self-knowledge.

So when you question the *what* of a job, remember the *why*. If you feel stuck in a job that you don't enjoy, a job that's unimportant, a job that's not respected by our culture's standards, focus not on *what* you do but on *why* you do it: To meet needs. To serve others. To serve God. To develop character.

Thank God every morning when you get up that you have something to do that day which must be done, whether you like it or not. Being forced to work, and forced to do your best, will breed in you temperance and self-control, diligence and strength of will, cheerfulness and content, and a hundred virtues which the idle never know. —CHARLES KINGSLEY

BORING, INSULTING, MONOTONOUS—AND THAT'S THE GOOD STUFF

An editor leaned across a conference table as if confiding a dark family secret to me. "My husband feels jealous of my job. Or maybe *jealous* isn't the right word. But I get to come to an exciting place every day to work. We print stories that change people's lives. We hear from our readers, and we get feedback, and we know that what we print makes a real difference in their lives. My husband's a graphic artist. He thinks what he does doesn't matter. That anybody could do it. That it has no lasting value. He says, 'Fifty years from now, who'll care that I designed their full-color brochure for under ten thousand dollars?' I try to reassure him that his work is important. He does lots of graphic design work for a big church in the area. Beautiful work. All gratis."

Many people echo the same idea. They consider their work boring, monotonous drudgery. Other people around them seem to have exciting work with eternal significance and impact. Fortunately for us, God didn't divide his workers into "significant" and "insignificant" categories.

Consider our construction metaphor: Builders who move from site to site, climbing ladders and framing the walls of one new house after another, may be tempted to view what they do as not particularly interesting or significant. They might be tempted to consider the electricians' work more significant because of the risk involved. Maybe they don't feel their work has as much impact because it is eventually hidden by plaster or drywall, wallpaper, paint, or tile. But if the framers don't see what they do as significant, just let them get sloppy on a few framing jobs. A few years later, the homeowners may begin to notice cracks developing, pictures not hanging straight, doors no longer closing snugly. As soon as we fall into the comparison trap, we lose the sense that what we do contributes significantly to the finished product. Judging what we do by cultural standards can leave us feeling as if we're trying to climb a shaky ladder: we're so focused on the ladder that we can't give all our energy to the task at hand.

> There is as much dignity in tilling a field as in writing
> a poem.
> —BOOKER T. WASHINGTON

Shaky Ladder #1: Those in "Ministry" Have Greater Value to God Than I Do

Brain surgeons and Tanzanian missionaries come with no higher recommendations from God than the graphic artist we heard about earlier. In fact, as Doug Sherman and William Hendricks point out in *Your Work Matters to God* (NavPress, 1987), if people enter the ministry simply because they want to be significant to God, they have a wrong motive. They would have made the same big mistake the blundering, thundering brothers James and John did when they requested the most prominent positions in God's kingdom (see Mark 10:35-37).

All God asks of us is that we be diligent and skilled: "Do you see a man skilled in his work? He will serve before kings; he will not serve before obscure men" (Proverbs 22:29). Then add an attitude to that skill base: "Daniel was preferred above the presidents and princes, because an excellent spirit was in him" (Daniel 6:3, KJV).

Attitude makes all the difference in doing significant work for God and others. Again, the why—the motivation—shines through.

Melvin Graham, younger brother of evangelist Billy Graham, shares his personal understanding of God's assignment for him. According to his comments during some of the Graham crusades, he used to be intimidated that his brother had preached before more than 210 million people in 185 countries—that is, until he fully understood that God had called him to be a farmer in North Carolina. Now he farms gladly and shares his faith with anyone who'll listen. He's living out his assignment, secure in the knowledge that his service has significance where God asked him to have significance—in his local sphere of influence.

God does not consider some of us more "significant" than others because of the work assignment he has given us to do. As long as we're doing what God has assigned, a minister has no greater reward in heaven than a software consultant does.

> If two angels were sent down from heaven, one to conduct an empire and the other to sweep a street, they would feel no inclination to change employments.   —JOHN NEWTON

Shaky Ladder #2: My Work Doesn't Have Significance or Lasting Value

Some people think that work that has a lasting value has more significance than work that will be around for only a day or a decade. Not true. God created both heaven (for forever) and earth (for here and now). God never said we were to ignore the now and focus only on the later. That would be quite impossible. Some jobs are meant to serve people and meet their needs now, in the present.

If you've been assigned to the here and now and your work has immediate value this week and next, why complain? God has not assigned you to second-class citizenship in the kingdom just because you're working "the first shift." Those whose work assignments last into the second shift (maybe the 2040 decade, if the world lasts that long) will hold no higher significance.

> *If I can put one touch of a rosy sunset into the life of any man or woman, I shall feel that I have worked with God.*
> —GEORGE MACDONALD

Shaky Ladder #3: All Work Should Be Eternally Meaningful

Drudgery and routine are part of any job. The CEO has to do a budget every single year to take to the board of directors. She has to plan a speech. She has to review the annual letter to the shareholders. Most CEOs will consider these functions the monotonous drudgery of their jobs.

A movie star will hate running lines and sitting in makeup for three hours.

A pro athlete will dislike running laps in one-hundred-degree temperatures after a four-hour scrimmage.

Jesus himself stooped to wash his disciples' dirty feet, and he cleaned and cooked their fish on the seashore. Neither of these tasks would have been "enjoyable." They were routine daily tasks that needed to be done. Of course, what Jesus was modeling about servanthood by his example had eternal significance, but the tasks themselves did not.

In our culture we tend to think every action must have a "significant," rather than a utilitarian, purpose. We want our meals as a family to be "conversational springboards." We want our vacations to be "bonding experiences." We expect our clients to give us "rave" feedback on our sales survey. We want our team members to bring up "gut-wrenching issues" that need to be resolved on our 360-degree feedback sessions.

Sometimes we need to stop and realize that everything will not be significant and meaningful—to *us*. To others, maybe yes. To us, maybe not. At times we see only our small slice of the project and lose sight of the bigger service we provide to others. Here's a case in point:

Suppose you're a stocker—you restock shelves in a greeting-card shop. You straighten the cards at ten in the morning, and they'll be a mess again at nine at night. How monotonous and meaningless—unless you think about the people who are deeply stressed over the serious illness of a friend. Those people have their minds elsewhere. They don't know whether to buy a card with a verse that's humorous, serious, religious, or says "just thinking of you," pretending their friend will get well when that may not be the case. Tense and worried, these customers rush into the store on the way to the hospital or the post office. You've made the selection much easier with the cards neatly organized, envelopes carefully matched and placed behind each card.

You may consider your stocking work menial, but customers may consider it significantly helpful because it meets an immediate need.

We can do no great things; only small things with great love.

—MOTHER TERESA

Shaky Ladder #4: My Employer Is Involved in Questionable Business Practices

In an era when "business ethics" sounds like an oxymoron, this shaky ladder can confuse and dishearten workers with high moral standards. Of course, when workers become aware of questionable or unethical business practices, they face tough choices about participating themselves and making others in authority aware of the situation.

But to lose heart about a job because you see business or your industry in general as questionable requires deeper thought about your direct participation and your motivation. Here are two key questions to ask yourself: (1) How direct are the links to questionable practices? And (2) are you serving others in your work in God's name?

Almost any business or industry you follow will eventually be involved in questionable practices somewhere down the line. Let's say you sell men's clothing at a local department store. Are you responsible if you sell someone a hat, jacket, and gloves and he later wears them to disguise himself during a robbery?

Let's say you own a small hardware store or a nursery. Are you responsible if someone uses tools or chemicals purchased at your store to kill a family member?

What if you own a chain of grocery stores that sells food and your primary customers in one city work in a sweatshop that pays substandard wages? Should you close down your grocery store so that the people who own and work at the sweatshop can't buy from you? Are you encouraging that business by keeping your own store open?

If you sell insurance, should you not sell it to the managers who work for the owner of the sweatshop? After all, if they couldn't get insurance for their families because they worked at that company, they'd eventually have to find another job and maybe eventually the manufacturer would have to go out of business because he had no managers.

It is difficult to draw the line, isn't it? The Bible says that God sends rain on both the righteous and the unrighteous (Matthew 5:45). He's not directly participating in the evil, but he's offering love to all. Can we do differently in our service?

> *The man who builds a factory builds a temple; the man who works there worships there; and to each is due not scorn and blame but reverence and praise.* —CALVIN COOLIDGE

THE LITTLE THINGS MAY BE THE MAIN ATTRACTION

The Kaleidoscope of Homes has become an annual event in the Dallas-Fort Worth area. Six or eight builders buy lots in a new development, build spec homes, and then open the homes to the public for a month to display the latest and greatest designs and gadgets. Their subcontractors generally do the work at very reduced fees for the opportunity to showcase their work on the tour that draws enormous crowds to the multimillion-dollar houses.

Because we were about to tackle remodeling our own home, we thought we'd take the tour one Saturday and stood waiting our turn to file into the guest bath while the couple in front of us *oohed* and *aahed* over something we couldn't yet see from our position outside the doorway.

The woman ahead of us glanced upward. "This is absolutely the best thing in the entire house. The very best thing."

Her husband agreed.

"Look at this. Just look," the woman continued. "You have to stand just a certain way or you can't see it at all. It's very subtle. The light has to hit it just right." She reached up to touch the "something" and flip the light switch. At that point the crowd moved on, and we were able to step inside the room to see the object of her delight. She pointed to a tiny shadow painted on the wall.

We edged past them and left them still standing in the bathroom, marveling at how the artisan had achieved the effect that could be seen only when the light was shining in a certain direction. In this two-million-dollar-plus house with original creations everywhere, this tiny imprint in the upstairs guest bathroom was the "best thing," the "main attraction" for this one couple. When we passed down the hallway ten minutes later, the same couple, plus others, still crowded into the guest bathroom to express their delight at the faint imprint on the wall.

Likewise, as you serve your colleagues, your customers, or your family, the very smallest acts that you may consider mundane may be the "main attraction" for them. Your friendly voice when you answer the phone may be their only connection with someone they consider a caring person.

Keith, a friend of ours, was surprised that his twenty-two-year-old daughter called him at work, because she typically saves personal calls for after hours. But her opening line was, "Dad, sorry, but I just had to hear a friendly voice for a minute or two. I get so tired of being screamed at all day long." She works in the credit department of an insurance agency.

You may be a corporate trainer, traveling from city to city, teaching people how to run software programs, ensure safety on oil rigs, or deal with conflict among coworkers. What you teach them may save their marriages, keep their teens from dropping out of school, prevent a crankcase explosion, or help them get jobs so that they can pay their monthly bills and provide food for their families.

To you it may be mundane, but to others it may be the main attraction.

> *When we hire employees, we don't care what their resumes say; we only care that they care.* —DEBBI FIELDS

You may be an administrative assistant who pushes paper, runs to this or that meeting, calms this or that upset client, books conference rooms or videoconferencing time, or untangles schedule conflicts. But your work may free several executives to concentrate creatively on a new product launch or to travel rested to a meeting with a new client or to go home and relax after a twelve-hour day, confident that you have things under control.

To you it may be mundane, but to others it may be the main attraction.

> *There is no future in any job. The future lies in the man who holds the job.* —GEORGE W. CRANE

Adding the Finishing Touches to Your Dream Home

Do you need panes in your windows, locks on your doors, studs in your walls, shingles on your roof, paint in your bedroom, faucets on your sink, tanks on your toilets? You probably don't particularly care whether these items win *oohs* and *aahs* from visitors. But you have them because they make your house functional, safe, and comfortable. You would never consider building a dream home without them.

You need to approach your work with the same mind-set: God's criteria for "meaningful" work makes almost all jobs serve his purposes.

When building Your Signature Work, understand that some parts of the structure may not be what they photograph for the Lifestyle section of the Sunday newspaper. Nevertheless, those parts—the door hinges, the electrical system, the rafters, or the water faucets—prove essential just the same.

When you're working as if God were your customer or your coworker, service makes sense and provides satisfaction on a deeper level. When you're faced with doing the mundane, value the here and now as well as the there and forever. Focus on the *why,* not on the *what.*

> If you are dissatisfied with your lot in life, build a service station on it.
> —SAMUEL BRENGLE

> The best way to appreciate your job is to imagine yourself without one.
> —UNKNOWN

> There are no menial jobs, only menial attitudes.
> —WILLIAM BENNETT

SEVENTEEN

WORKING ON THE WIRING
Are You Shining Brightly—or Shorting Out?

*D*o your peers consider you a primary contributor or a slacker?

*W*ould your customers, colleagues, or family members agree that you work with integrity?

ABOUT a month after we moved into our new house, we noticed a squeaky board in the hallway. Down on hands and knees, we checked the floor. Surely we hadn't already damaged it in some way without realizing it, had we? No pets. No kids at home. No heavy furniture. Closer examination showed no sign of a scratch. Just a squeak. A few days later, when the board popped up, we called the builder.

"No problem," he said. "I'll just send the subcontractor back over to nail it down again."

A few days later, another squeak. Another board popped up, this time in the kitchen. Then another in the hallway. Another in the breakfast area. After about six months, our floorboards were popping like popcorn. But the builder had grown tired of sending the subcontractor over to nail them down. For the next two years we begged, we pleaded, we cajoled.

At this point the builder responded, "So sue me," and then declared bankruptcy, only to "rise again" as a different business entity. The subcontractor did the same. We finally had to resort to a lawsuit against them personally to get action on replacing the hardwood floor. In preparation for the case, as various experts paraded in and out of our house and we took photos while they removed the ruined floor, the problem became evident. The workmen had failed to nail the wood down properly during installation.

Their shoddy work cost the builder and subcontractor about twice what it would have cost (considering floor repair and reimbursement for our legal expenses) if they had done the job correctly the first time. And all of us involved would have saved a lot of time and headaches. The replacement floors may have shined brightly, but the builder's and subcontractor's work ethic did not.

Have you ever been the victim of a roof that leaked? a foundation that cracked? wallpaper that peeled? plumbing that backed up because the pipes were improperly installed? a payment miscredited? a legitimate insurance claim payment long overdue? a prescription mislabeled? If so, then you understand the frustration of having to deal with mediocre work.

SIGNING THE CHECKS VERSUS *CASHING* THE CHECKS

Sometimes the difference in your perspective about productivity and excellence stems from whether you're *writing* the check or *cashing* the check. That is, are you *paying* for the product or service or *delivering* the product or service? Are you paying for a good day's work, are you providing a good day's work? Are you the customer or the seller? Are you suffering the consequences of someone else's mediocre performance or attitude, or are you the person who's doing less than excellent work?

"These weekends are killing me," Carey (not her real name) laughed. "I was up late Friday night—drove to Shreveport for a ball game. Then Saturday we had an all-day retreat and stayed up all night. Gone all day Sunday. I'm exhausted. I can't wait till I get back to the office Monday morning to rest!"

Unfortunately, she was serious. And she did—rest, that is. Almost every Monday she took the entire day to recuperate from the exhausting weekends she spent leading activities for singles—sporting events, retreats, and miscellaneous speaking engagements around the state. On the following Fridays she got little work done in the office because she was using her day to make calls, plan, and prepare for her weekend of church activities. According to her coworkers, she put in about three days of work each week and took home a paycheck for five.

Is low productivity a growing problem? As you walk through the break room or the company cafeteria, you'll likely hear tidbits of conversations regarding what your colleagues are doing, have been doing, or plan to do during their day on the job: Laura's sending a cartoon, a poem, and three quotations to thirteen friends and colleagues. Bryan's checking his investment portfolio to discover he's lost another two thousand dollars over the weekend. Kevin's surfing travel-related Web sites for a quick getaway trip over a long weekend to surprise his wife for their tenth anniversary. P. T. is tracking Michael's last move on the electronic chessboard. Su Lin is ordering Christmas gifts for her nine grandchildren from four different shopping sites. Sedrick is gathering sports results from the second-rate games that he didn't find time to tune in to over the weekend. Carlita is sending a note to her three sisters that their brother will be in town next week and would like to plan a get-together for dinner whichever night they're all free. And by the way, has anybody heard when the family reunion will be taking place next month? If so, please get back to her about the details and let her know where to find cheap airline tickets.

On average, non-work-related Internet surfing and e-mail use cost American businesses 54 billion dollars and a 30 to 40 percent loss in productivity every year. Businesses lose an estimated 26 million worker hours each year to employee game playing alone, according to a study by the Gartner Group.

Let's bring it a little closer to home, with information from several studies done by business consultants from the Gartner Group, American Management Association, and Yankelovich Partners. According to the U.S. Department of Labor, the 2002 mean hourly wage for all nonsupervisory workers in nonfarm jobs was $14.93 per hour. For all civilian workers in white-collar

Hourly Worker Cost—All Nonsupervisory, Nonfarm Workers (doubled to cover benefits, etc.)	$29.86
Daily Nonbusiness Use	1 hour
Daily Cost	1 x $29.86 = $30 (rounded to nearest dollar)
Weekly Cost	5 x $30.00 = $150
Annual Cost per Worker (based on 2,080 hours)	52 x $150.00 = $7,800
Annual Cost per 1,000 Employees in the Company	1,000 x $7,800.00 = $7,800,000

Hourly Worker Cost—All White-Collar Workers (doubled to cover benefits, etc.)	$41.24
Daily Nonbusiness Use	1 hour
Daily Cost	$1 x $41.24 = $41 (rounded to nearest dollar)
Weekly Cost	5 x $41 = $205
Annual Cost per Worker (based on 2,080 hours)	52 x $205 = $10,660
Annual Cost per 1,000 Employees in the Company	1,000 x $10,660 = $10,660,000

jobs, the mean wage and salary was $20.62 per hour. To determine the full hourly cost for an employee, taking into account benefits, work space, and so forth, we double the hourly wage. The national average for nonbusiness Internet use is one hour per employee per day.

If every employee surfs the Internet or uses e-mail for personal communication for an hour a day, the cost is 12.5 percent of the overall company's payroll. It adds up.

That's not the end of the problem, of course. Leisure surfing clogs up the network access and prevents real work use. Additionally, legal issues surface when objectionable e-mail and Internet material is introduced into the workplace. But the personal productivity issues alone create questions in the minds of observers: Do these employees understand what they're doing—or not doing—on the job?

Many, like Carey, just don't have their hearts and minds focused on the day's mission. They haven't considered how honesty relates to productivity. They *are* productive—but only about their own personal interests, not necessarily what they're accepting a paycheck to accomplish.

Folks who never do any more than they get paid for, never
get paid for any more than they do.   —ELBERT HUBBARD

Sometimes nonproductivity stems from other causes. A
pastor friend gave the personnel committee this explanation for
dismissing a church staff member: "He's simply lazy. He com-
plained about occasionally having to work forty-five hours a
week. He always counted Sunday and Wednesday church services
as part of those hours when our regular church members add
those hours on top of their regular work week. In fact, I cau-
tioned him that he better not complain about having to work
a forty-five-hour week in front of any church members—they'd
laugh in his face. Other professionals who take home his salary
are typically working fifty-five to sixty hours a week."

If heaven is a place to rest, many people are going to be all
practiced up for it.   —UNKNOWN

In short, this pastor was saying, too many people are ready
to carry the cue sticks when it's time to move the pool table.

If you want to know whether the members of a work crew are
being paid by the hour or by the project, just watch them a few
minutes, and you'll soon figure it out. When we built our first
house years ago, we developed the following theory, based on our
own observations. After checking with the general contractor,
our theory turned out to be sound in every case. Here's what we
observed:

If we dropped by the house and the workers were scurrying
around busily and efficiently, they invariably were being paid by

the project. As subcontractors they had bid a certain amount to do framing or painting or landscaping or to install Sheetrock, and they were getting the job done so they could move on to another. They were doing it well, also, because they knew if it wasn't done correctly, the general contractor would hold them responsible, and they'd have to come back and correct the problem.

If when we dropped by, we found workers standing around watching each other, doing things in a slipshod way, or not verifying their work against the blueprints, invariably we discovered that these people weren't the subcontractors but only the crews. They worked by the hour. If they didn't get the job done today, they'd be paid again for working on it tomorrow. If the job wasn't done right, they didn't have to cover the repair or replacement cost out of their paychecks.

On a much bigger scale that same mentality surfaces in stockbrokerage firms, software companies, oil fields, and pharmaceutical research companies. Productivity flows down to individual accountability.

The productivity problem presses close to physical, psychological, and spiritual issues. Physical causes for lower productivity include various handicaps or illnesses that make walking or moving difficult, such as crippling arthritis or multiple sclerosis, or a heart condition. These are understandable and excusable.

But the psychological and spiritual causes of low productivity reveal issues that need attention.

- dishonesty about doing a day's work for a day's pay
- anger and a "get even" mentality directed toward an employer, a customer, a team leader, or a supervisor

- anger and a "get even" mentality directed toward coworkers from those who must "pick up the slack"
- ingratitude toward God for health, skills, and the opportunity to work and provide for one's needs
- laziness

A lazy person has trouble all through life.

—PROVERBS 15:19, NLT

Productivity has become the name of today's competitive game. Unfortunately, some people haven't suited up to play. But the lack of productivity is nothing new. People through the ages have always belonged to one of five categories: (1) those who always do *less* than they're asked, (2) those who do *just* what they're asked, (3) those who do *more* than they're asked, (4) those who do things *without* being asked, and (5) those who *rally others* to do more than they're asked.

Each of us chooses our own category. And each of us reaps the benefits or consequences of that choice.

So what's the "norm," or standard? That depends on whom you ask. Some employees think working any more than forty hours a week is excessive and should generate a bonus, overtime pay, or at the very least, high praise. Some business owners think working anything less than seventy hours a week shows a lack of dedication on the part of employees. Both of these positions are extremes.

Biblical evidence suggests that a six-day workweek was the norm—work six days and then take a day of rest. But the larger issues remain accomplishment, results, and attitude—not clocked time.

"Lazy hands make a man poor, but diligent hands bring wealth," according to Proverbs 10:4. But wealth has a broader context than simply money. Productive people become rich in personal satisfaction, influence, and results. A sense of accomplishment makes people feel worthwhile, that what they do matters. Nothing makes you feel more tired than putting in a long day at work and then leaving at the end of the day feeling as though you had started dozens of projects and finished none of them. Productivity is a source of personal fulfillment.

> *I never remember feeling tired by work, though idleness exhausts me completely.*
> —FICTIONAL DETECTIVE SHERLOCK HOLMES

The result of your productivity is, of course, another reward for your effort. And finally, a by-product of your diligence is that others take notice of successful people around them. When you accomplish things, it's only natural that you gain "clout" with coworkers and clients. You earn a reputation as a go-to person. What you say carries weight. Your opinion counts. Your behavior sets the standard.

So, we know what kind of behavior earns the respect of others, but what causes people to lose respect for a coworker or colleague or friend?

> *There are an enormous number of managers who have retired on the job.*
> —PETER F. DRUCKER

PACKING THE LEAST WORK INTO THE MOST HOURS WITH MINIMAL KNOW-HOW

Some people lose the respect of their friends and coworkers because of their lack of productivity for what seems like a more forgivable cause: Their lack of productivity is not related to laziness; instead, these people lack good habits. They create conflict in the absence of clearly established priorities. They communicate poorly. They fail to plan and instead react from crisis to crisis. They try to get things done in a disorganized work space, amid clutter and chaos.

> *Don't tell me how hard you work. Tell me how much you*
> *get done.*   —JAMES LING

Now stir in minimal training, an average aptitude for the job, a big ego, and a low tolerance for feedback, and you have a recipe for mediocrity. Instead of shining brightly at what they do, these people tend to short out when it comes to work performance.

Longevity is no longer enough. Effort alone doesn't earn a paycheck in today's environment. Executives, business owners, and customers alike want to pay only for solid performance. Coworkers expect each other to add enough value to the team or the project that if any of them leaves, something significant will be missing.

Workers who add value operate like independent contractors and think like owners. They see the big picture, eliminate unnecessary steps and processes, avoid turf battles, cut costs where possible, and do what it takes to get the job done right. They're accountable for results—not just the time expenditure.

> *Take a lesson from the ants, you lazybones. Learn from their*
> *ways and be wise!*   —PROVERBS 6:6, NLT

THE RESIDENT CYNIC AND WHINER

Walk through the company cafeteria in almost any organization in the country and you'll often hear someone talking about low morale. Who's responsible for it. How it's affecting "everybody." How to improve it. The ancient list of seven deadly sins referred to it as "sloth"—a rebellion of the spirit, a protest against the divine order of things (politicians, executive management, or whoever's in charge), an "I don't know, and I don't care" attitude. The *Merriam-Webster Collegiate Dictionary,* tenth edition, defines *sloth* as "disinclination to action or labor, . . . apathy, inactivity." Modern-day individuals with this mind-set call themselves cynics. Colleagues call them whiners.

Cynics reflect an inner despair and listlessness. Everything seems meaningless; nothing merits trust; nothing summons attention. Excitement and idealism have escaped them. They are bored, burned out, bottomed up.

Cynics haven't mastered their moods or morale. On the job they complain that executives can't be trusted. Salaries, vacation, and benefits are inadequate. Client demands are irrational. Customers are stupid. Coworkers are incompetent. Suppliers are slick. The government is lying. Nothing is as it seems. There's no way out. All is hopeless. Those who are enthusiastic about their work are "suckers" who get trapped for trying.

The only difference between complainers and cynics is degree—the depth of their despair and the hardness of their hearts.

Cynics have stopped drawing a line between the temporary and the permanent. They believe that bad days will not pass; they are forever. And they've shunned taking any personal responsibility for their mind-set.

Granted, every day of every job is not fun and games. Ask talk-show hosts if they enjoy responding to their e-mail. Ask senators if they like haggling in a committee meeting at two in the morning or traveling all night on a campaign swing through the state. Ask pro athletes how exciting it is to do 17 "takes" of a TV commercial for a sponsorship deal. Ask the president if he likes having Secret Service agents hanging around when he wants to kiss his wife. Ask the corporate CEO if he enjoys taking phone calls from irate stockholders or responding to questions from angry board members. Ask business owners how exciting it is to deal with venture capitalists.

Some days, according to motivational speaker and entrepreneur Charlie "Tremendous" Jones, the real work may be finding a way to put excitement into your work. It's a mission he takes seriously. At seventy-five, with a business to run, he still works twelve- to eighteen-hour days, finds time to pursue his passion for entertaining inner-city children at his Pennsylvania farm, and flies all over the country on weekends to speak to corporate, church, or community groups.

Does he have cause to be a cynic? For starters, he gives away a fortune every year—financial donations, books from his publishing business, time to charitable causes. And yet he has been struggling with cancer for the past few years, and to top that off, a trusted employee put his company in serious financial trouble until Jones discovered the situation. So yes, he could lay claim to cynicism if he wanted to snuggle up close. But that's neither his demeanor nor his dogma. You'll never meet a more passionate, joyful CEO than Charlie.

One of the biggest problems with cynics who can't manage their morale is that their condition is contagious. Carriers can infect a crowd quite quickly. And the spiral for cynics and the people around them swirls downward faster and faster. The problem is that they give up personal accountability, and in blaming others for the reasons for their cynicism, they're stripping themselves of power.

Those on United Flight 93 could have given in to despair on September 11, 2001. But they did not. In the face of sure loss of life, they took control of the situation and overpowered their captors to save lives on the ground. The world saw what people can do to change bleak circumstances when they are determined to exercise personal courage and their character refuses to give in to a mind-set of cynicism.

There's nothing chic about cynicism. Whining does not win friends and influence people.

Enthusiasm is like a ripple in water, it grows.

—KENNETH GENTLE

"CLOSE ENOUGH" FOR GOVERNMENT . . . UH, CHURCH . . . CHARITY . . . VOLUNTEER WORK

Have you heard this line: "It's close enough for government work"? Although many talented, dedicated government officials have worked hard to overcome that stigma, impressions linger for a long time. In fact, rather than disappear, that sentiment seems to have morphed into other arenas: church work, charity work, or any volunteer work that goes unrewarded by a paycheck.

Some people particularly equate the idea of "no pay" with "no effort." That is, anything that's done on a voluntary basis gets a halfhearted effort at best. For community, church, or civic responsibilities or projects, they use leftover time, leftover resources, leftover supplies, and leftover energy. If things don't turn out well, the attitude seems to be, "Oh, well, it was a voluntary effort. What did they expect?"

But this mind-set, too, flies in the face of biblical teaching: "Work hard and cheerfully at whatever you do, as though you were working for the Lord rather than for people," says Colossians 3:23 (NLT). It's biblical to keep balance in our lives. It's biblical to rest. It's biblical to say no to a project. But it's not biblical to accept a job—paid or volunteer—and do it with mediocrity.

MADE IN THE USA—A PROUD SHIVER OR A BAD QUIVER?

Does this label—Made in the USA—on a product cause you worry or give you peace of mind? Or is it meaningless until you know the companies and individuals involved? When a product or a service reflects poor quality—whether for fee or for free—the defects defraud others.

Here's a slice of our experience in gathering initial bids for our house remodeling project: We call Fred, a painting contractor with multiple crews, and set up an appointment for him to come out and give us a bid. He shows up on a Tuesday morning, measures the rooms, and tells us he'll fax his bid the next day. The following Monday, when we still don't have his bid, we phone his office.

No return call. One week later, we leave another voice mail, on his cell phone. This time he returns the call. "So sorry. But I do have your bid ready. I'll just give you the amount now over the phone." Which he did.

"The amount sounds fine. Would you fax your quote so we'll

have it in hard copy today? Then we'll let you know something by the end of the week."

The fax never arrives that day. When his quote still hasn't come on Thursday (sixteen days after our original meeting), I leave another voice mail.

He responds by voice mail to say he "doesn't understand what has happened with the faxed quote but that he will mail the quote to us. On the following Monday (now twenty-one days after our initial appointment), I phone to say that neither the faxed nor mailed quote has arrived and that we plan to make a decision that day.

He drives over and drops the quote in our mailbox without an explanation about why neither the U.S. Postal Service nor his fax seems to work. We also note that the price has been raised from what he'd quoted on the phone. I review the copy dropped in our mailbox and leave him a voice mail saying that I have a couple of questions.

Seven more days pass (now twenty-eight days after our initial meeting), and Fred still has not called to answer my questions. Despite receiving good references from friends about the work Fred did on their house, we give up on him. I leave him a voice mail to tell him that obviously he has more business than he can handle and that we have selected another painter to do the work.

Within an hour, Fred calls. He said he's had a death in the family and has been out of town all week.

His explanation might still have given us second thoughts had I not known the truth: The day of our first meeting I had passed along his name to my parents, who also needed painting done. During the week he'd supposedly been out of town, he had set an appointment with them, missed that appointment, and then spent a second afternoon at their house—all while he was "out of town" attending a funeral.

Is the way Fred runs his business an oddity? Is this lack of shining performance confined to one industry? Think about your own experience: Have you eaten at restaurants where surly staff members served stale, cold food? Have you stayed at hotels where management seemed to be doing you a favor to let you check in when they were "so busy" or gave you a lecture about "arriving so late"? Have you purchased shoddy products that didn't work long enough to get them home? In fact, how many items do you have that are defective? Does this line from the manufacturer or store clerk sound familiar? "Might as well buy a new one. It'll cost you more to repair it than to buy a new one."

If slogans helped, we'd be guaranteed first-class everything. Just read the ads. Listen to the commercials. Look at the brochures: "We're dedicated to quality." . . . "Service is our middle name." . . . "Your satisfaction guaranteed." Far too often these are only empty promises. Some quality problems can be attributed to a system problem or a process itself. But other times quality issues can be attributed to a lack of quality work on the part of an individual. It just takes one singer in the quartet to make the entire group sound off-key.

It's easy to see why quality has taken a nosedive:

- There is little or no accountability for actions or inactions. We're lightly supervised. Often the boss is located elsewhere. We work over the Internet, and no one "sees" what we do. We may be more technically savvy than the boss, and he or she doesn't understand whether or not we do things right.

- There are few consequences for poor quality. The length of time we stay in a particular job seems to grow shorter and shorter. We make decisions and then move on before we have to live with the bad situations or consequences we create by those decisions.

- Many organizations show little or no sense of loyalty to their workers, even laying them off at the drop of a hat to make the year-end financial statements look good. They may have protected senior executives with "golden parachutes" but given little thought to the average worker's dwindling retirement account.

- Customers show no loyalty to suppliers who've helped them through tough start-ups; then they feel justified when the quality of a supplier's product slips.

In short, people fail to understand that they're building their Signature Work for God, not for each other, and based on his principles, not on their own justification.

A defective product or poor service reflects weak character. Being responsible for such products and services—as the manufacturer, designer, salesperson, service agent, or company owner—puts you in a precarious position of mediocrity.

LOOKING FOR YOUR LUCKY LOTTO?

The get-rich-quick mentality afflicts both the haves and the have-nots. It causes people to take their minds off of today's ball game to focus on something "out there" that never seems to materialize but always manages to mess up their current relationships and jobs. The Bible warns about get-rich-quick schemes: "He who works his land will have abundant food, but he who chases fantasies lacks judgment" (Proverbs 12:11).

The Bible has no problem with people trying to make money. The more money you have, the more you can give away to good causes. But the get-rich-quick mentality the Bible warns about is the mind-set that wants to make tons of money with little or no effort, without regard for how it's done or who gets hurt in the process. For a list of practices that plague our common land-scape, consider these:

- swallowing up other business, pushing the assets into a parent organization, leaving the liabilities for a shell organization, and then declaring bankruptcy
- investing money in ventures you don't understand or haven't investigated thoroughly
- risking money you can't afford to lose on long-shot deals
- participating in schemes that allow you to make your money back but leave others holding the bag

The common motivator in all of these is greed. Customers may buy from you and colleagues or coworkers may work with you under such conditions, but they usually do so without passion—without engaging their hearts and souls in their work.

Adding the Finishing Touches to Your Dream Home

Who would you rather have building your dream home: a certi-fied master builder or a mediocre general contractor who's pick-ing up odd jobs in his or her spare time, buying "seconds" on lumber and supplies, and subcontracting only with the lowest bidders? Chances are, you would want the best your budget will allow.

In whatever job you do, coworkers, supervisors, clients, customers, or friends want and expect the best. Mediocrity motivates few.

As you build Your Signature Work, the biggest trap to avoid is falling into the murkiness of mediocrity where the masses spend their time. If your work habits tend to short out, your clout and influence will grow dim. But if your efforts reflect excellence, your results will shine.

> *Iron rusts from disuse, stagnant water loses its purity and in cold weather becomes frozen; even so does inaction sap the vigors of the mind.* —LEONARDO DA VINCI

> *Even those who do nothing that can be called work still imagine they are doing something. The world has not a man who is an idler in his own eyes.* —W. HUMBOLDT

EIGHTEEN

CHECKING THE ROOF
Protecting the Parts That Make Up the Whole

*W*hat's distinctive about your work?

*D*oes your attitude toward your work repel or attract others?

*H*ow strong is your influence on those around you?

MORE than sixty guests wandered around the terrace and toured all three floors of the mansion overlooking Puget Sound and Vancouver Island in British Columbia. We focused on the Rembrandt over the mantle, the Louis XIV chandelier, the color-coordinated closets and drawers laid out like those in designer boutiques, the indoor pool and accompanying locker suites for men and women, the cooks' quarters, and the travel treasures or artifacts showcased in various niches. We were guests of business professionals and philanthropists Joe and Rosalie Segal.

After the guests were seated at tables of eight in the foyer and waiters had taken our entrée orders for the evening, someone commented to the host about the satisfaction he must feel about the rewards of his labor and his obvious business acumen and success.

"I'd give it all up and start over," our host responded, "just to have a clear runway."

"A clear runway?" someone asked.

"I'm seventy-eight years old. I have just a few years left. I'm at the end of life's runway. Most of you here are in midlife. You still have another twenty, thirty, forty years of runway." He gestured toward the opulence around him and continued reflectively, "I'd give it all up—go back to work, start over with nothing in my bank account—just to have a chance to live life . . . over again. I've loved every minute—the working part."

Joe and Rosalie have certainly made a name for themselves all over Vancouver, British Columbia, for their generosity to many charitable causes and their leadership among many organizations and groups. They host two or three charitable functions a month in their home.

Certainly their lifestyle is distinctive. It causes people to ask how and why. How did they accumulate such wealth? And why, at their age, do they continue to put themselves to so much trouble? They have no need to impress people, to win business, or to network to gain friends. Why, then, are they so generous with their money, time, and energy?

The answer doesn't really matter—the fact that people repeatedly ask the question is the point. The Segals have worked and lived in a way that makes people take notice. They have a platform. When they speak, people listen.

> *The career of a great man remains an enduring monument of human energy. The man dies and disappears, but his thoughts and acts survive and leave an indelible stamp upon his race.*
> —SAMUEL SMILES

WHAT'S DISTINCTIVE ABOUT YOU?

As you build Your Signature Work, what's distinctive about you? What makes people ask how and why about the way you approach your work? Or do they?

Today's greatest need is for a distinctive lifestyle in our workplace, whether it's an office, a classroom, our home, a construction site, a research lab. That's where we spend our time and rub elbows with other people long enough for them to see what we're made of. Our lifestyle and leadership there should pique others' interest enough to make them ask why and then whet their appetite for the same influence, results, and satisfaction.

Consider for a moment how you determine the architectural style of a house. If, like me, you're not a student of architecture, you may have to study carefully to determine the style of a particular house: What kind of roof does it have? Does it have several gables or none? Does it have plantation shutters and a front porch that wraps around three sides, or large windows with no trim accessories at all? Finding the answers to such questions can help you to identify the architectural style.

Just as we determine a house's style by looking at various parts that make up the whole, we come to understand individuals in the same way. Five key attitudes or behaviors tell others what you are on the inside and show you to be either distinctive or commonplace in the work world:

- your choice of work
- your attitude about life and your lifestyle in general
- your approach to your work
- your treatment of others
- your response to moral issues

Looking at each of these five key characteristics separately will help you to evaluate whether you are distinctive or commonplace where you do your work.

> *My grandfather once told me that there are two kinds of people: those who do the work and those who take the credit. He told me to try to be in the first group; there was much less competition there.* —INDIRA GANDHI

Your Choice of Work

- Does your work provide for your needs and/or your family's needs in an honest way or a dishonest way?
- Does your work help others or contribute to their downfall?

Your Attitude about Life and Your Lifestyle in General

- What values do you reveal?
- How do you relate to others? to your community? to God?
- Do you reflect a positive faith?
- How do you respond to crises? tragedy? disappointment? success?
- Do you live with integrity and consistency?
- Is your lifestyle attractive to others and satisfying to you?

Your Approach to Your Work

- How competent are you? Do you use your skills and talents to their fullest?
- Do you do the best job possible with dedication, energy, and enthusiasm?
- Do you show restraint about overwork? "Do not wear

yourself out to get rich; have the wisdom to show restraint"
(Proverbs 23:4).

- Do you respect authority? "Submit yourselves for the
  Lord's sake to every authority instituted among men"
  (1 Peter 2:13).
- Do you put first things first, prioritize, plan, and lay a
  proper foundation in your work and in your personal life?
  "Finish your outdoor work and get your fields ready; after
  that, build your house" (Proverbs 24:27).
- Do you manage your time well?

> *Promises must be kept, deadlines met, commitments
> honored; not just for the sake of old-fashioned morality, but
> because we become what we do (or fail to do) and character
> is simply the sum of our performances.*   —UNKNOWN

Your Treatment of Others

- Do you treat others with dignity? Are you impartial to
  others on a social and intellectual level when you meet?
  "Show proper respect to everyone" (1 Peter 2:17).
- Are you kind and compassionate?
- Do you do good to and for others when you can? How?
  When? "Do not withhold good from those who deserve
  it, when it is in your power to act" (Proverbs 3:27). That
  "good" may include giving people who deserve them
  positive performance ratings, raises, words of praise,
  recognition for a job well done, referrals for business,
  help with projects. Be sensitive to opportunities to meet
  others' needs—physical, emotional, spiritual.

- Do you mediate conflict rather than cause it? "Reckless words pierce like a sword, but the tongue of the wise brings healing" (Proverbs 12:18).
- Do you guard against angry words? Are you a problem solver? "A gentle answer turns away wrath, but a harsh word stirs up anger" (Proverbs 15:1).
- Do you give negative performance feedback privately? Reprimanding others openly shows disrespect and dramatically diminishes chances the individual will be able to focus on any corrective action.
- Do you avoid gossip?
- Do you refrain from expressing outward hostility or using put-downs that sound humorous but are really intended to embarrass or convey disrespect and harm others' careers?
- Do you forgive when conflict arises?
- Do you build positive relationships with coworkers, suppliers, customers?
- Do you follow through and honor your commitments to others? Work settings would operate on an entirely different level if people called when they said they would, showed up at meetings they confirmed, forwarded paperwork they promised, and responded to e-mails. Those who are dependable show respect for others who trusted what they say.
- Do you show fairness in all dealings?
- Do you hire applicants honestly by not misrepresenting the job they applied for? Do you avoid making promises that create false expectations and rob people of opportunities they may have had elsewhere and may never have again?
- Do you represent accomplishments and qualifications for

jobs and promotions honestly so that employers do not miss opportunities they might have had with other candidates?

- When you delegate projects or tasks and plan to hold others accountable for the results, do you also give them the necessary resources and authority to accomplish the tasks? Delegating responsibility and accountability without authority shows a lack of trust.
- Do you pay your bills and your creditors as you have agreed?
- Do you pray for others—those who may oppose you as well as those who support you?
- Do you offer counsel to those who ask for your advice?
- Do you share your faith in a way that is appropriate to your personality and the situation?

> *The simple act of paying positive attention to people has a great deal to do with productivity.*
> —TOM PETERS AND ROBERT WATERMAN JR.

Your Response to Moral Issues

- Do your work ethic and the integrity of your values undercut or invalidate your words?
- Do you even notice immorality or questionable practices?
- Do you participate in them?
- Do you express opposition to them?
- Do you demonstrate and suggest alternatives to the immoral option?

All of these work habits show up as character issues that either build or destroy credibility. They are all parts that make up the whole of Your Signature Work.

Just as dishonest builders declare bankruptcy and resurface under different names to compete again with honest builders, . . . just as shady mortgage companies take advantage of unsuspecting buyers right beside fair lenders who offer solid financing to home owners, . . . dishonesty and disrespect leave tracks in every workplace.

As peers, subordinates, bosses, or customers observe or discover these things, they form judgments about your relationships, values, character, faith, and an entire range of related issues.

The solid gain a platform. The shady lose their opportunity to influence.

> *A faithful employee is as refreshing as a cool day in the hot summertime.* —PROVERBS 25:13, TLB

Lest you think we don't or can't possibly reveal all these things about ourselves in our daily encounters at work, consider this brief conversation between Darla and coworker Jody at lunch:

"I'm leaving for lunch a few minutes early," Darla tells Jody. "If my husband calls, tell him I've gone to lunch. Alone. And don't just put him into voice mail. Tell him he's got to get to the bank to make a deposit. They've called to say we're overdrawn *again*. And I'm *not* making the deposit."

"Sure. Will do," Jody says.

"And don't tell him when I left."

"Okay." Jody makes a note of what Darla has asked her to remember for the expected phone call.

Darla gathers up her coat and umbrella and heads out the

door. "If I had any guts at all, I'd head out of this place and just keep driving."

"Hey, you want me to finish the registration form for that Atlanta conference while you're gone?" Jody calls after her.

"No, just wait. I'm not sure when I'm going to leave. I may decide to go a day or two early to visit a friend who lives there. I could tell my boss they had a preconference session or something that I needed to attend. He's too stupid to figure it out. And if I asked him for time off, he's such a jerk that he wouldn't let me go."

"Isn't that the week you have to conduct all the performance appraisals for your new recruits?" Jody asks.

"Oh, you may be right. I forgot to put that on the calendar. There's probably a note there somewhere in the pile about that—when I get time to dig it out. Just leave the registration. I'll handle that myself when I get back. Or next week. I can't stay late tonight. I've got to get to yoga class, and then we're having dinner at the club at eight."

From this brief exchange that you might easily have overheard from the office next door, what have you learned about Darla? It's quite revealing what a few snatches of conversation here and there convey about someone's values, lifestyle, and relationships. In addition to overhearing conversation, we get copied on e-mails, observe others in meetings, hear one-sided phone conversations with a mother or a spouse, see how others dress, observe the hours they work or don't work, learn how dependable they are, discover how they spend their money, experience their moods, hear their philosophies, hear how they spend their leisure time, and see how they contribute to their communities and churches.

Very little gets lost.

> We look into mirrors but we only see the effects of our times
> on us—not our effects on others.   —PEARL BAILEY

PLUMBERS AND PHYSICIANS WITH PLATFORMS

Roger McBride's Signature Work has earned him the right to be heard. The first time he came to our house to repair the washing machine, he investigated the problem and shook his head. "I could replace this motor, but several other parts look worn. You want my advice? Junk this and buy a new machine."

"Okay. Thanks for your honesty. We'll do that. How much do we owe you for today's call?"

"Nothing this time. I wasn't able to help you."

"But you made a trip out here."

"No problem. I was in the neighborhood already. I don't charge unless I do work. Just remember to call me next time." And with that, he was gone.

Another time Roger was too busy to do our plumbing project himself. He had taken a full-time job that left him free to do his handyman work only on weekends, so he referred us to a relative just getting started in the business and guaranteed his work. "He'll do a good job. And if there's anything not done just right, you call me, and I'll take care of it."

Roger's friend came and did the job—a mediocre one. His role in our remodeling effort was to replace the existing bathroom fixtures with a new toilet and a new pedestal sink. On closer inspection, we discovered that the toilet was cracked around the base and the sink was glued to the wall crooked. When we confronted him about the messy job, he merely shrugged his shoulders, denied any knowledge of how the toilet got cracked, and insisted that the wall rather than the sink pedestal was crooked.

Roger to the rescue. On his second day off after working twelve-hour days, seven days a week, for two months (his company was moving into new facilities and demanded overtime from all maintenance staff), Roger showed up at our door, plumbing tools in hand. Why? Because he had guaranteed the other guy's work. Roger worked from nine in the morning until he finished redoing the botched job just before midnight. And he refused to accept any payment, saying that we had already been overcharged for the work the first time around.

Not long ago a neighbor called Roger about his mother's air conditioner. "Mother called a service technician out—someone from the yellow pages. He told her she needed a new unit and it was going to cost her four thousand dollars. Would you mind going by there and checking it out just to be sure before she signs the contract for them to install it?"

"Sure thing," Roger promised his neighbor.

He discovered that the woman had fallen victim to an all-too-common scam on the elderly. The technician had disconnected a few wires that caused the air conditioner to stop cooling. All Roger had to do to "repair" it was to reconnect the wires, add Freon, and clean the filters. He appeared to be as irate at the technician as he would be if the customer had been his own mother.

When we've mentioned that we don't think Roger charges enough for some projects—in comparison to what others have charged us in the past—he has always responded, "I know what the parts cost me. I know how long it really takes to repair things. It's a fair price. My reward for honesty will come in heaven."

Roger's general outlook on life, his honesty, his attitude, and his dependability make his work distinctive. He attracts people to his faith, and he has earned a platform in his sphere of influence.

On the other hand, Jay McFee (not his real name), is a marketing specialist at a large engineering firm in Chicago. He's outspoken about his Christian beliefs and often reads his Bible in the company cafeteria during his lunch hour. On Monday mornings, when others in the employee lounge are talking about their wild parties or trips, he frequently talks about his weekend church activities.

Yet it's not uncommon to overhear Jay behind closed doors in a shouting match with his marketing director over how to handle marketing campaigns in his region. In staff meetings Jay belittles his boss in front of the group when a marketing campaign doesn't generate the number of leads expected. In fact, Jay uses thinly veiled sarcasm to embarrass his boss in front of the senior executives at every opportunity.

Respect for authority has not entered his consciousness in connection to his faith and leading a distinctive lifestyle. Colleagues overhearing the shouting matches frequently wonder about the disconnection between the two. When Jay brings up matters of faith and tries to influence others on moral issues, his comments don't hold water.

To go back to our construction metaphor once again, if homeowners don't check the roof regularly and give attention to any loose shingles, those weak areas will allow rainwater to soak into the wood underneath. Over time those leaks can cause cracks in ceilings and walls and eventually undermine the integrity of the entire structure. Jay hasn't understood that his failure to take care of each part of his character has undermined the whole of the Signature Work he's trying to build. As a result, his integrity is weakened, and he has lost his platform for having a positive influence on those around him.

> *What you are thunders so loud that I cannot hear what you say to the contrary.* —RALPH WALDO EMERSON

Like Roger McBride, Dr. Ron Yamamoto, an orthopedic surgeon, has a firm platform and a solid roof. He does his Signature Work primarily on knees—and on hearts. Affable, highly skilled, and committed to his patients, Dr. "Yam" rarely treats patients without taking an opportunity somewhere in the surgery cycle to give them a Bible. He has a roomful of Bibles— a variety of colors, translations, sizes, study guides—to offer those who don't have their own. The teenage athletes in particular respond to his simple message of faith because he takes the time to show an interest in their sports and in them as individuals while he treats their physical condition and prays for their healing.

Dr. Wally Rhine, at Clearview Eye Clinic, performs eye surgery for patients who could otherwise not afford it. This action alone speaks volumes about his own vision and values.

Phil and Lillie Romano, owners of restaurant chains such as Fuddruckers and Macaroni Grill, feed thousands of homeless people each year with their Hunger Busters soup-kitchen-on-wheels. With soup from one Romano restaurant and sandwiches from another, they go to the back streets of Dallas two nights a week and deliver food mixed with hope.

Whatever your title, assignment, or work, others are watching you. Make sure that you swing the right tools—with precision and excellence—and that the sun shines through your attitude.

> *People are won to your religious beliefs less by description than by demonstration.* —UNKNOWN

Adding the Finishing Touches to Your Dream Home

The easiest business comes by referral. Homebuyers often select a general contractor, an architect, and an interior decorator because of the results these professionals have produced for others. If their finished work looks good, the prospective buyers start to "ask around" for answers to questions about behind-the-scenes details.

The same is true in other fields and on your job. When others are attracted to your workplace personality and performance, you generate "referrals" for your faith and gain opportunities to exercise leadership on a larger scale.

People want to follow a leader in the same way sports fans want to root for a winning ball team or homebuyers want to sign a contract with an award-winning builder. Likewise, if your work style looks distinctive and your attitude attracts others rather than repels them, those people will ask why and how. You've then earned the right to be heard about your goals, values, beliefs, and faith. As a result, your solid roof protects what you've built, your platform grows, and your influence spreads.

> *Preach all the time, and every once in a while, if necessary, use words.*   —ST. FRANCIS OF ASSISI

> *The Christian ideal has not been tried and found wanting. It has been found difficult; and left untried.* —G. K. CHESTERTON

> *You should be a light for other people. Live so that they will see the good things you do. Live so that they will praise your Father in heaven.*   —MATTHEW 5:16, ICB

NINETEEN

ADDING PERSONAL TOUCHES
Finding Satisfaction in What You've Built

*I*s the ideal job a reality or a figment of modern society's imagination?

*A*re you a success? How do you know?

*D*o your time commitments and results match your values and bring you personal satisfaction?

WE DIDN'T think the question we posed to Carol, the first interior decorator we interviewed, was all that difficult. "Our Realtor told us that if we intend to sell the house for top dollar, we need to change the gray carpet to beige. So we'd like to have your opinion on that and any other suggestions for changes."

Carol made a quick walk-through of the house and gave us the following recommendations:

1. Change the gray carpet to beige.
2. Paint the walls a slightly darker taupe, but keep everything neutral.

3. Replace and update all the wallpaper in the bathrooms and the kitchen.
4. Replace the drapes in the dining room.
5. Add drapes in the formal living room.
6. Replace the bedspread and drapes in the master bedroom.
7. Paint the stained cabinets in the bathrooms all white.
8. Leave the library alone.
9. The upstairs is "hopeless," so just forget it, and concentrate on the downstairs to make the sale.

We posed the same question to Ray, the second decorator. Here is his list of recommendations:

1. Change the gray carpet to a pale green to go with the granite in the kitchen.
2. Paint the walls various shades of pale green to go with the carpet. All neutrals would be boring.
3. Keep the wallpaper in the kitchen and three bathrooms and replace the wallpaper in the remaining baths.
4. Keep the drapes in the dining room.
5. Add only sheers in the formal living room.
6. Keep the bedspread and drapes in the master bedroom; they are the best thing in the room. We'll work with those to "rebuild" the room.
7. Keep the stained cabinets as they are—no paint.
8. Redo the library. Re-cover the chairs, paint the iron staircase, and add new carpet.
9. The upstairs looks simple and fine.

Decorator number three, Jan, was our favorite. After reviewing her list, you'll understand why.

1. Keep the gray carpet. It's perfect with the cool tones of the furniture.
2. Don't repaint. The white walls look fine with the gray carpet.
3. Replace the wallpaper only in one bath.
4. Keep the drapes in the dining room.
5. Don't add sheers in the formal living room—your open contemporary look works well.
6. Replace the bedspread and drapes in the master bedroom.
7. Keep the stained cabinets in the bathrooms as they are.
8. Leave the library alone. It looks cozy and has personality.
9. Just move the furniture around upstairs. No need to buy anything new.

After decorators four and five came and made their suggestions, they left us thoroughly befuddled. As we reviewed the suggestions from each decorator to determine which one we wanted to work with, we came to one major conclusion: Evidently, "house beautiful" is in the eye of the beholder. So why not choose the décor *we* liked because we would be the ones to live in our house until it sold?

The same can be said of the work life you're building. Ultimately, you must decide whether your work is both satisfying to you and pleasing to God. But all too often, as we did with the decorators, people listen to too many uninformed opinions about which schools to attend, college majors, glamorous job offers, and tempting promotions. And along the way, circumstances and situations occur that create confusion on the job and make us weary and wishy-washy, even in well-doing.

For example, maybe the circumstance that grabs our attention is a money crunch at home, a spouse's dislike of our job responsibilities, cultural attitudes about our work, a bad boss, or unsupportive colleagues. Or possibly we get laid off, downsized, or merged to the point that we're without a paycheck and at a loss as to where to look next.

In the soul-searching that happens between jobs, we often ask the deeper questions that we don't have time to consider when we're working nine to five: Am I in the right job? Do I really enjoy my work? Is God trying to teach me something? Am I being stubborn?

Possibly the most common cause of confusion is imbalance—the pull between the passionate enjoyment of your work and the love of your family and other pursuits. If you enjoy your work and feel called to it and understand that it's a way to reflect your sense of God's calling, isn't more work better?

Well, that depends. Frustration sets in when work starts to crowd out other things we believe and value. Take, for example, these perplexities:

We value time with our children, but we travel in our job. We want to provide well for our family. Paying for the finest education for our children requires putting in extra hours at work—which means we have less time actually to *spend* with our children.

We enjoy spending time with our spouse, yet our weekends are filled with running errands in opposite directions just to get "caught up" and ready to go back to work again the next week.

We value good health, but we can't find time to exercise because of our long work hours. So we eat unbalanced meals that add calories without nutrition and, as a result, often feel tired and sick.

We value the emotional support from friends, but we never have time to carry on intimate conversations about real problems and issues in our lives or about purposeful, fulfilling pursuits.

We believe that good citizens participate in government, yet we don't have time to study the platforms and voting records of those running for office and seldom have time to volunteer in political or community causes because our work assignment requires all our emotional involvement.

> *I'm living so far beyond my income that we may almost be said to be living apart.* —SAKI (HECTOR HUGH MONRO)

In these dilemmas the theoretical is at war with the practical. That is, theoretically you love both your family and your job and should have appropriate time for both. But practically speaking, your daily activities don't measure up to what you intended at the start of each week, month, or year. In short, the reality of how you spend your time doesn't match your vision and values for your overall life.

Is there such a thing as the ideal job, or is that a figment of our modern society's imagination? Instead of feeling angry and resentful that somehow we got shortchanged, we need to do a reality check more often. Few perfect jobs exist outside human resources journals or job descriptions listed under "To Be Created." In any job, hectic days and weeks produce frustration—if we look only at that one slice of time.

But as investors in the stock market know, we have to take a long-term view. And we have to decide to change what we can control. We *can* make changes.

People who have successfully realigned time and activity with their values say they have accomplished or learned the following:

- They understand the true trade-off between time and money.
- They are "doing" some of their dreams.
- They feel freedom.
- They feel relief from pressure.
- They feel guiltless.
- They have deeper relationships with their spouses, children, and friends.
- They live within their financial means and feel less financial stress.
- They have more time for self-development projects and learning.

All of these changes stem from attitudes and basic drives. To change the work life you're building, you have to change the idea that you have control. You have to break away from a mentality of "searching" so that you can catch a glimpse of what balance and contentment look like.

If your work brings satisfaction, overwork will not necessarily bring ecstasy. Instead, overwork may be the needle that bursts the bubble of joy.

FROM RESTLESSNESS TO CONTENTMENT

Restlessness feels like an itch that you can't scratch. We look around and think that promotions aren't coming fast enough.

Salary increases aren't hefty enough. Recognition isn't visible enough. The learning isn't broad enough. What we consider "enough" rarely has a standard definition.

Sometimes restlessness ripples through our consciousness as we compare our work and our lifestyle to those of our friends, family, or neighbors. We drive through the neighborhood and see people walking their dog at eleven on Thursday morning and wish we could work from home—until we miss the camaraderie of friends at the office and the fun of going out for lunch with them. We envy our neighbors' vacation trips to Paris or Hawaii or Rome—until we realize that both adults work in excess of sixty hours a week and leave their children with sitters during those hours to be able to afford those vacations. We dream of owning our own business, controlling our own destiny, and reaping the rewards of our labor—until we discover the long hours, the financial risks, and the emotional investment. We long for the no-pressure eight-to-five job with no headaches—until we need a bigger paycheck.

Comparisons, without the complete picture, kill contentment. I'm not advocating complacency, however, which the *Merriam-Webster Collegiate Dictionary,* tenth edition, defines as "self-satisfaction accompanied by unawareness of . . . deficiencies." Henry Ward Beecher observed: "If a man has come to that point where he is so content that he says: I do not want to know any more, or do any more, or be any more, he is in a state in which he ought to be changed into a mummy." Complacency marks the end of growth—spiritual, personal, professional.

Content makes poor men rich; discontent makes rich men poor.
— BENJAMIN FRANKLIN

Goals and striving mark the difference between complacency and contentment. Complacent people have no goals, no desire to improve. Content people experience satisfaction and fulfillment where they are but still have goals and a desire to grow. Someone has summed it up well with this distinction: Be content with what you *have* but never with what you *are*. Always work on becoming. "Godliness with contentment is great gain. For we brought nothing into the world, and we can take nothing out of it" (1 Timothy 6:6-7).

Personally, professionally, and spiritually, a complacent person has closed up shop while a content person is always open for business.

> *The Lord is my shepherd; I have everything I need.*
> —PSALM 23:1, NLT

Contentment is a big step on the way to gratitude. Contentment often results from your choice to trust God as the judge of your present and the creator and caretaker of your future.

FROM NEED TO GREED TO GRATITUDE

Both the rich and the poor struggle with financial issues. The poor may lie awake and worry about how to pay their bills, resent the fact that others make more than they do, and feel that they are underpaid for what they do. The rich may worry about paying too many taxes, agonize about whether they are being cheated in business deals, and fear losing everything they've worked so hard to earn if the economy takes a nosedive.

Maybe the cure for those worries, whichever group you're in, is to remember the following well-known statements: When someone asked John D. Rockefeller Sr. how much money it takes to make people happy, he replied, "Just a little bit more."

The second comment has been variously attributed to John D. Rockefeller, J. P. Morgan, Aristotle Onassis, and John Jacob Astor, depending on who's telling the story. Obviously, it originated with only one and has been borrowed or erroneously attributed by others, but it nevertheless makes the point well. After the wealthy individual died, a reporter asked the lawyer settling the estate, "How much did he leave?" Answer: "All of it."

Compared to those in other countries, we Americans consider ourselves generous to our fellow human beings around the globe in times of tragedy. But as a population of individuals with one of the highest standards of living in the world, our average charitable giving amounts to a paltry $1,050 per income tax return, or about 2.2 percent of adjusted gross income. What we make, we like to hang on to for ourselves.

Those who preach a prosperity gospel say, "If you're in God's will, you'll be healthy, wealthy, and wise." But the teachings of the Bible as a whole don't bear this out. The writer of Proverbs 30 knew the value of moderation: "Give me neither poverty nor riches, but give me only my daily bread. Otherwise, I may have too much and disown you and say, 'Who is the Lord?' or I may become poor and steal, and so dishonor the name of my God" (Proverbs 30:8-9). In other words, if we have too little money, we may stoop to dishonesty and dishonor God. If we have too much, we may begin to think we don't need God in our lives. The apostle Paul, too, admonished us against letting greed drive our work life: "Keep your lives free from the love of money and be content with what you have" (Hebrews 13:5).

There are two things needed in these days; first for rich men
to find out how poor men live; and second, for poor men to
know how rich men work.   —JOHN FOSTER

The desire for more drives our work lives to the brink of
chaos. Once our true basic needs are met, we begin to focus
on wants. To put an end to the continual striving for more and
to keep work hours manageable and have energy left to devote
to other important pursuits, many people have decided to
simplify their lifestyles. They have decided that after they have
enough to live comfortably and to meet their basic needs, they
will invest the rest of their money in other people and causes
outsides themselves—with gratitude for the opportunity to
work at something they love.

Store up for yourselves treasures in heaven, where moth
and rust do not destroy, and where thieves do not break
in and steal.   —MATTHEW 6:20

Where your treasure is, there your heart will be also.
                                        —LUKE 12:34

HOW DO YOU SPELL SUCCESS?

Every profession has its own symbols of "success." To athletes,
it's an Olympic medal. To movie stars, it's taking home an
Oscar. To a politician, it may be a chance to sit in the Oval
Office. To singers, it may be the chance to perform at Carnegie
Hall. To an accountant, it's making senior partner in the firm.

To a consultant, it's landing the top client in the industry. To a manager, it's becoming CEO. To a stay-at-home parent, it's a well-equipped, well-adjusted child grown to adulthood.

When it comes to life in general, however, people disagree about what constitutes success, according to a 2002 survey conducted by the Barna Research Group. One-fourth of the survey respondents defined personal success in terms of tangible outcomes or accomplishments such as wealth, educational achievement, or having made significant contribution to the world. One-third (32 percent) cited the health and well-being of family and a solid marriage. And one-fourth had no idea what would indicate that they had lived a successful life.

Unless you know from the outset how you—and God—will measure your success, you'll likely teeter back and forth on this balance issue as the cultural winds blow.

As long as you feel unsuccessful in your job by God's standards, you may tend to overwork and throw the rest of your life and the lives of your family members out of balance in many other ways. You shortchange them and even your church and your community by giving them less of your time and energy than they deserve.

If, on the other hand, your goal is to pursue a life of leisure and happiness as a primary goal outside your work, you may miss the very thing that brings you the most fulfillment.

Realize that true happiness lies within you. Waste no time and effort searching for peace and contentment and joy in the world outside. Remember that there is no happiness in having or in getting, but only in giving. . . . Happiness is a

perfume you cannot pour on others without getting a few drops on yourself.
                         —OG MANDINO

The following are some measurements of work success others have found helpful through the centuries:

Emotional Satisfaction from a Job Well Done

When God finished the work of creation, he looked at the results and said, "It is good." If you feel the same satisfaction about the work you do, count yourself fortunate. If you are doing your best and are receiving positive feedback on your work, that's a good indication that you are succeeding at what you do. On the other hand, if at the end of the day or week you feel as though you've been spinning your proverbial wheels and have turned in a lackluster performance, you will feel drained, empty. And if what you feel about your performance is true, then over time, others will probably even confirm your lack of competence and poor performance.

Enjoyment and Fun

Gaining a sense of satisfaction from doing a job well is not necessarily the same thing as loving what you do. Some people would do what they do even if they didn't get paid for it. That is true of me as a writer and was true of my husband, Vernon, in his role as an Army reservist for nineteen years after active duty. Failure, on the other hand, in contrast to success, will be marked by a lack of passion for your work.

Achievement

Working toward a significant goal, learning, developing your skills, and building character as you deal with people or problems on the job produce personal satisfaction. When you are experiencing success, you probably also experience moments of happiness along the way toward accomplishing a goal. On the other hand, if you are achieving no goals, no growth, and no gain, it will likely be evidence of failure.

> *Achievement is the knowledge that you have studied and worked hard and done the best that is in you. Success is being praised by others, and that's nice, too, but not as important or satisfying.* —HELEN HAYES

Financial Provisions

If you earn a paycheck for what you do, it may be a measure of success in that it says you have the skills, talent, discipline, and character necessary to earn a living. In other words, others recognize these gifts or traits in you and are willing to give you money in exchange for your exercising them.

Money to Give Away

If you earn enough money to meet the needs of your family and still have excess to give away and invest in other people, causes, or ministries, that is an additional measure of success and a source of satisfaction. With this measurement, however, the converse may not be true: If the economy is weak and you are truly struggling to make ends meet, that is not necessarily a sign that you are a failure. If you are going through hard financial times or a time of unemployment and are unable to contribute to other causes or ministries for a time, that's not an indication of failure. God knows whether your heart is willing even when your resources are meager.

Godly Influence

No matter what work you are called to do, you can reflect your faith in God in that work. You may get to see the results of your influence more often in some jobs than in others. You may even receive immediate feedback on your impact, and those open, verbal acknowledgments may give you great satisfaction. They should also lead you to gratitude for the opportunities God gives you to have such influence.

> *There are many ways to measure success; not the least of which is the way your child describes you when talking to a friend.* —THE BIG BOOK OF GOD'S LITTLE INSTRUCTIONS

You may want to add your own measures or symbols of success. But remember that you don't have to add another layer to your life to please God. Spending your time building Your Signature Work produces satisfaction that comes no other way.

> *Learn to be pleased with everything; with wealth, so far as it makes us beneficial to others; with poverty, for not having much to care for; and with obscurity, for being unenvied.*
>
> —PLUTARCH

Adding the Finishing Touches to Your Dream Home

It seems that some homeowners are never satisfied. They trade up every few years to a bigger house, a better neighborhood, a shorter commute. Then once they're "there"—wherever "there" is—when their children grow up and leave or when the home-owners retire, they begin to move "down" to a smaller house, less yard to maintain, a lot on a lake, or a city nearer the grandkids. Circumstances change. Wishes wander. Some homeowners rarely stay still.

That same restlessness invades us from time to time in our work. We may wake up one morning and wonder, "Am I happy here? Am I successful? Should I move on to something else?"

Be wary about the restlessness that has reached epic propor-tions in many work environments today, the sense that if you're not changing jobs or moving up or on every year or so, you're a failure. Take care, too, against the other extreme: losing your balance and overworking for whatever reason—either for the love of money, the love of other symbols of success, or the love of your job.

Instead of working to earn something, work to *become* something. Work to become fulfilled. Work to become useful to others. Work to reflect God's character on earth.

The ideal job rarely exists in reality. But you can build Your Signature Work on a vacant lot very close to it.

A man's life does not consist in the abundance of his possessions.   —LUKE 12:15

Contentment is something that depends a little on position and a lot on disposition.   —UNKNOWN

Work is the medicine of the soul.   —GRENVILLE KLEISER

There are far too many people in the world who live without working, and far too many who work without living.

—DIOGENES

A FINAL NOTE

Your own Signature Life is a work in progress. You may be discouraged by the difference between your vision of your finished masterpiece and the work you've completed thus far. But don't dwell on your failures, unrefined skills, or undeveloped themes. Instead, focus on the time remaining, the character still to be shaped, the scenes still to be created, the design still to be modified, and the building still to be done.

When your masterpiece is completed, sign it with care. God will be the final appraiser.

RESOURCES BY DIANNA BOOHER AVAILABLE
FROM BOOHER CONSULTANTS

BOOKS: Selected Titles

Speak with Confidence: Powerful Presentations That Inform, Inspire, and Persuade

E-Writing: 21st Century Tools for Effective Communication

Communicate with Confidence®: How to Say It Right the First Time and Every Time

Fresh-Cut Flowers for a Friend

Little Book of Big Questions: Answers to Life's Perplexing Questions

Get a Life Without Sacrificing Your Career

Good Grief, Good Grammar

To the Letter: A Handbook of Model Letters for the Busy Executive

Great Personal Letters for Busy People

The Complete Letterwriter's Almanac

Clean Up Your Act: Effective Ways to Organize Paperwork and Get It Out of Your Life

Executive's Portfolio of Model Speeches for All Occasions

The New Secretary: How to Handle People as Well as You Handle Paper

Writing for Technical Professionals

Winning Sales Letters

Ten Smart Moves for Women

Get Ahead, Stay Ahead

The Worth of a Woman's Words

Well Connected: Power Your Own Soul by Plugging into Others

Mother's Gifts to Me

The Esther Effect

Love Notes: From My Heart to Yours

First Thing Monday Morning

VIDEOS

Writing for Results

Writing in Sensitive Situations

Building Rapport with Your Customers

Giving and Receiving Feedback Without Punching Someone Out!

Thinking on Your Feet: What to Say During Q&A

Basic Steps for Better Business Writing (series)

Business Writing: Quick, Clear, Concise

Closing the Gap: Gender Communication Skills

Cutting Paperwork: Management Strategies

Cutting Paperwork: Support Staff Strategies

AUDIOS

Get Your Book Published

People Power

Write to the Point: Business Communications from Memos to Meetings

E-LEARNING PROGRAMS

Selling Skills and Strategies: Write Proposals That Win the Business

Selling Skills and Strategies: Thinking on Your Feet: Handling 11 Difficult Question Types

Selling Skills and Strategies: Write to Your Buyers: E-mail, Letters, Reports

Selling Skills and Strategies: Create and Deliver Sales Presentations with Impact

Selling Skills and Strategies: Negotiate So That Everyone Wins

Selling Skills and Strategies: Everyone Sells: Selling Skills for the Non-Salesperson

Selling Skills and Strategies: Manage Your Pipeline, Accounts, and Time

Effective Writing

Effective Editing

Good Grief, Good Grammar

More Good Grief, Good Grammar

Ready, Set, NeGOtiate

WORKSHOPS

E-mail Excellence™

Effective Writing

Technical Writing

Developing Winning Proposals

Good Grief, Good Grammar

eService Communications

Communicate with Confidence®

Customer Service Communications

Presentations That Work® (oral presentations)

Listening until You Really Hear

Resolving Conflict without Punching Someone Out

Leading and Participating in Productive Meetings

Negotiating So That Everyone Feels Like a Winner

Increasing Your Personal Productivity

Managing Information Overload

SPEECHES

Communicate with Confidence®: From Boardroom to Bedroom

Communicate with Confidence®: The 10 Cs

The Gender Communication Gap: "Did You Hear What I Think I Said?"

Communicating CARE to Customers

Write This Way to Success

Platform Tips for the Presenter: Thinking on Your Feet

Get a Life Without Sacrificing Your Career

You Are Your Future: Putting Together the Puzzle of Personal Excellence

The Plan and the Purpose—Despite the Pain and the Pace

The Worth of a Woman's Words

Ten Smart Moves for Women

FOR MORE INFORMATION

Dianna Booher and her staff travel internationally presenting programs on communication and delivering motivational keynote addresses on life balance and personal productivity topics. For more information please contact:

Booher Consultants, Inc.
2051 Hughes Road
Grapevine, TX 76051
Phone: 817-318-6000
mailroom@booher.com
www.booher.com

ABOUT THE AUTHOR

DIANNA BOOHER, Certified
Speaking Professional (CSP),
is an internationally recognized
business communication expert
and the author of forty-one books
and numerous videos, audios, and
Web-based e-learning products for
improving communication, sales
effectiveness, and productivity. She is the founder and president
of Booher Consultants, based in the Dallas-Fort Worth
Metroplex. The firm provides keynote addresses on life balance
and personal productivity, and communication training (written,
oral, interpersonal, gender, customer service) to some of the largest Fortune 500 companies and government agencies, among
them: ExxonMobil, Lockheed Martin, IBM, GlaxoSmithKline,
Kraft, Caterpillar, PepsiCo, Frito-Lay, Nokia, J. C. Penney,
Morgan Stanley, Ernst & Young, Texas Instruments, and the
Army and Air Force Exchange Service. *Successful Meetings* magazine recently recognized Dianna in their list of "21 Top Speakers
for the 21st Century." Dianna holds a master's degree in English
and was recently inducted into the Speakers Hall of Fame.

Dianna and her husband, Vernon, also a member of Booher
Consultants, have two grown, married children and live in Texas.